Super Easy ROS Python

James Hunter

Chapter 1: Introduction to ROS

ROS (Robot Operating System) is a set of software libraries and tools that provide hardware abstraction, low-level device control, sensor data processing, high-level control, message-passing between nodes, and package management. It's not an operating system in the traditional sense like Windows or Linux, but rather a collection of tools that enables rapid development of robot applications.

ROS provides a framework for:

- Managing hardware abstraction: ROS allows you to write device drivers once, and use them across multiple platforms.
- Sensor data processing: ROS offers a variety of libraries for processing sensor data like images, laser scans, GPS feeds, etc.
- High-level control: ROS enables you to develop complex behaviors using high-level programming languages like Python.
- Message-passing between nodes: ROS uses a publish/subscribe mechanism for real-time communication between different nodes in the system.
- Package management: ROS follows a package-based structure that helps organize code and dependencies effectively.

1. **Real-Time Communication**: ROS facilitates real-time communication between nodes using topics (a named buffer to which nodes can publish messages) and services (a mechanism for blocking communication).

2. **Hardware Abstraction**: ROS allows you to write device drivers once, making it easier to switch between hardware platforms.

3. **Modularity**: ROS follows a modular structure with packages that contain code and dependencies. This makes the system extensible and maintainable.

4. **Open-Source**: ROS is open-source, meaning it's free to use, modify, and distribute. It has a large community contributing to its development and maintenance.

5. **Multi-Language Support**: ROS supports multiple programming languages like C++, Python, JavaScript (with rosbridge), Lisp (with CL-ROS), and others through bridges.

History and Evolution of ROS

ROS was initially developed by Willow Garage in 2007 to address the challenges faced while developing software for robots. It was designed to be open-source, modular, and extensible. After Willow Garage shut down in 2013, the ROS project was spun off into an independent foundation called Open Robotics.

Over the years, ROS has evolved significantly with contributions from a large community of developers worldwide. The current version is ROS 2 (Robot Operating System 2), which is designed to be more modular, scalable, and robust than its predecessor.

Understanding Nodes, Topics, Messages, and Services

Nodes

In ROS, a node is the basic unit of execution. It's essentially a program that runs on your machine. Each node has a unique name within the ROS namespace. Here's an example of creating a simple node using Python:

```python
import rospy
from std_msgs.msg import String

def talker():
    pub = rospy.Publisher('chatter', String, queue_size=10)
    rospy.init_node('talker')
    rate = rospy.Rate(1)  # 1 Hz
```

```python
    while not rospy.is_shutdown():
        hello_str = "hello world"
        rospy.loginfo(hello_str)
        pub.publish(hello_str)
        rate.sleep()

if __name__ == '__main__':
    try:
        talker()
    except rospy.ROSInterruptException:
        pass
```

Topics

Topics in ROS are named buffers to which nodes can publish messages. They serve as a communication channel between nodes. In the example above, 'chatter' is a topic.

Messages

Messages are the data structures used for communication between nodes. They are defined using .msg files and can contain various data types like int32, float64, string, etc. For example:

```
# Fibonacci.msg
int32 n
```

In this case, n is an integer value that can be published or subscribed to.

Services

Services are a mechanism for blocking communication between nodes. Unlike topics which use a publish/subscribe model, services allow one node to request data from another and wait for a response. Here's an example of a service definition:

```
# Fibonacci.srv
int32 n
```

---

int32[] output

In this case, the server receives n as input and returns an array of integers (output) as output.

The Role of Python in ROS Development

Python is one of the most commonly used languages for ROS development due to its simplicity and readability. ROS provides extensive support for Python through packages like rospy (for ROS 1) and rclpy (for ROS 2).

Here's an example of a simple Python script that subscribes to the 'chatter' topic:

```python
import rospy
from std_msgs.msg import String

def callback(data):
    rospy.loginfo("Received: %s", data.data)

def listener():
    rospy.init_node('listener')
    rospy.Subscriber('chatter', String, callback)
    rospy.spin()

if __name__ == '__main__':
    listener()
```

In this chapter, we've covered the basics of ROS, including its key features, history, and core concepts like nodes, topics, messages, and services. In the next chapters, we'll delve deeper into these concepts and explore how to use Python for ROS development.

Chapter 2: Setting Up the Environment

In this chapter, we will guide you through setting up your environment for working with ROS (Robot Operating System) using Python. We'll cover installing ROS and its dependencies, configuring catkin workspaces, installing Python-specific ROS libraries like rospy, and testing your setup with example packages.

Installing ROS and Python Dependencies

Before proceeding, ensure you have a modern Linux distribution installed on your system, as ROS is primarily designed for Ubuntu. For this guide, we'll use Ubuntu 20.04 LTS (Focal Fossa).

1. **Update your package list:**

```
sudo apt update && sudo apt upgrade
```

2. **Install ROS Noetic Ninjemys (Ubuntu 20.04 LTS):**

```
sudo apt install ros-noetic-desktop-full -y
```

3. **Initialize rosdep for installing system dependencies:**

```
sudo rosdep init
rosdep update
```

4. **Install required Python packages:**

ROS provides the python-rosinstall-generator package to generate a workspace with Python-based ROS packages. Install it along with other essential Python dependencies:

```
sudo apt install python3-rosinstall-generator python3-colcon-common-extensions python3-vcstool -y
```

5. **Install rospy, the Python binding for ROS:**

```
pip3 install rospy
```

Catkin is a build system that integrates with ROS and CMake, making it easy to manage dependencies between packages.

1. **Create a catkin workspace:**

mkdir -p ~/ros_catkin_ws/src
cd ~/ros_catkin_ws/
catkin_make

2. **Source the workspace setup file:**

source devel/setup.bash

Setting Up the Environment with rosdep and source

To work efficiently in your ROS environment, you need to set up your workspace and source it correctly.

1. **Navigate to your catkin workspace:**

cd ~/ros_catkin_ws/

2. **Source the setup file:**

source devel/setup.bash

Now, whenever you open a new terminal or start a new shell session, make sure to source your workspace:

source ~/ros_catkin_ws/devel/setup.bash

Testing the Installation with Example Packages

Let's create and test a simple ROS node using Python to ensure our environment is set up correctly.

1. **Create a new package:**

```
catkin_create_pkg hello_world rospy std_msgs
cd src/hello_world/
```

2. **Modify CMakeLists.txt** to include the following lines:

```
find_package(rospack)
parse_arguments(hello_world arguments LINKED_LISTS)
set(hello_world_catkin_DEPENDS rospy std_msgs)
```

3. **Create a Python script (scripts/hello_node.py):**

```python
#!/usr/bin/env python
import rospy
from std_msgs.msg import String


def hello_world():
    pub = rospy.Publisher('chatter', String, queue_size=10)
    rospy.init_node('hello_world', anonymous=True)
    rate = rospy.Rate(1) # 1 Hz
    while not rospy.is_shutdown():
        greeting = "Hello ROS!"
        rospy.loginfo(greeting)
        pub.publish(greeting)
        rate.sleep()


if __name__ == '__main__':
    try:
        hello_world()
    except rospy.ROSInterruptException:
        pass
```

4. **Make the script executable:**

```
chmod +x scripts/hello_node.py
```

5. **Build your workspace:**

```
cd ~/ros_catkin_ws/
catkin_make
```

6. **Run your node:**

```
rosrun hello_world hello_node.py
```

7. **Verify the node's output:**

Open another terminal and run:

```
rostopic echo /chatter
```

You should see messages like this:

```
data: "Hello ROS!"
```

Congratulations! You have successfully set up your ROS environment with Python support, created a package, and tested it using a simple example.

In the next chapter, we will explore how to create more complex packages and work with ROS messages and services.

Chapter 3: ROS Nodes and Topics

In this chapter, we delve into the core concepts of ROS (Robotic Operating System) nodes and topics using Python with the rospy library. You'll learn how to create ROS nodes, publish and subscribe to topics, and establish inter-node communication. We'll also discuss best practices for structuring your Python nodes.

Writing ROS Nodes in Python

To create a ROS node in Python, you first need to initialize a node using the rospy.init_node() function. Here's a simple example:

```python
import rospy


def main():
    # Initialize the node with a unique name
    rospy.init_node('my_node')

    # Your node's code goes here

if __name__ == '__main__':
    try:
        main()
    except rospy.ROSInterruptException:
        pass
```

In this example, we've created a simple ROS node named my_node. The try-except block ensures that the node can be interrupted cleanly when the user presses Ctrl+C in the terminal.

ROS uses a publish/subscribe model for inter-process communication. Nodes publish messages to topics, and other nodes subscribe to those topics to receive messages. Here's how you can implement this in Python:

Creating Publishers

To create a publisher, use the rospy.Publisher constructor with the topic name and message type as arguments:

```python
import rospy
from std_msgs.msg import String


def main():
    # Initialize the node
    rospy.init_node('publisher_node')

    # Create a publisher for strings on the 'chatter' topic
    pub = rospy.Publisher('chatter', String, queue_size=10)

    rate = rospy.Rate(1)  # 1 Hz

    while not rospy.is_shutdown():
        msg = "Hello, ROS!"
        pub.publish(msg)
        rospy.loginfo(f"Published message: {msg}")
        rate.sleep()


if __name__ == '__main__':
    try:
        main()
```

```python
    except rospy.ROSInterruptException:
        pass
```

In this example, we create a publisher for strings on the 'chatter' topic and publish messages at a rate of 1 Hz.

Creating Subscribers

To create a subscriber, use the rospy.Subscriber constructor with the topic name, message type, and callback function as arguments:

```python
import rospy
from std_msgs.msg import String


def callback(msg):
    rospy.loginfo(f"Received message: {msg.data}")


def main():
    # Initialize the node
    rospy.init_node('subscriber_node')

    # Create a subscriber for strings on the 'chatter' topic
    sub = rospy.Subscriber('chatter', String, callback)

    rospy.spin()


if __name__ == '__main__':
    try:
        main()
    except rospy.ROSInterruptException:
        pass
```

In this example, we create a subscriber for strings on the 'chatter' topic and log any received messages using the callback function.

Now let's combine publishing and subscribing to demonstrate inter-node communication:

Node 1 (Publisher):

```python
import rospy
from std_msgs.msg import Int32


def main():
    # Initialize the node
    rospy.init_node('publisher_node')

    # Create a publisher for integers on the 'counter' topic
    pub = rospy.Publisher('counter', Int32, queue_size=10)

    count = 0
    rate = rospy.Rate(1)  # 1 Hz

    while not rospy.is_shutdown():
        msg = count
        pub.publish(msg)
        rospy.loginfo(f"Published message: {msg}")
        count += 1
        rate.sleep()

if __name__ == '__main__':
    try:
        main()
    except rospy.ROSInterruptException:
        pass
```

Node 2 (Subscriber):

```python
import rospy
from std_msgs.msg import Int32

def callback(msg):
    rospy.loginfo(f"Received message: {msg.data}")

def main():
    # Initialize the node
    rospy.init_node('subscriber_node')

    # Create a subscriber for integers on the 'counter' topic
    sub = rospy.Subscriber('counter', Int32, callback)

    rospy.spin()

if __name__ == '__main__':
    try:
        main()
    except rospy.ROSInterruptException:
        pass
```

In this example, Node 1 publishes integers on the 'counter' topic at a rate of 1 Hz, while Node 2 receives and logs those messages.

Here are some best practices to follow when structuring your ROS nodes in Python:

1. **Keep nodes small and focused**: Each node should have a single purpose or responsibility.

2. **Use meaningful names**: Choose clear, descriptive names for your nodes, topics, and messages.

3. **Avoid global variables**: Instead, use class attributes or arguments to pass data between functions.

4. **Error handling**: Always handle exceptions that can be raised by ROS or Python libraries.

5. **Log messages**: Use rospy.loginfo(), rospy.logwarn(), and rospy.logerr() to provide feedback about your node's operation.

6. **Use rate.sleep()**: Ensure your node doesn't consume excessive CPU resources by using rate.sleep() in your loops.

By following these best practices, you'll create more maintainable, robust, and efficient ROS nodes in Python.

Chapter 4: ROS Messages and Services

In this chapter, we will explore two fundamental concepts in ROS (Robotic Operating System): messages and services. These are crucial for enabling communication between different nodes in a ROS system.

ROS uses messages to facilitate communication between nodes. You can define your own message types using the msg files in the msg folder of your ROS package. Here's how you can create and use a simple custom message called Person.msg:

```
# Person.msg
string first_name
string last_name
int age
```

To generate Python classes for this message, you can use the rosmsg command:

```
rosmsg gensrv --py Person.srv PersonService.py PersonService_pb2.py
```

Now you can import and use this message in your Python scripts:

```python
from Person.msg import Person

# Create a Person message
person = Person()
person.first_name = "John"
person.last_name = "Doe"
person.age = 30

# Publish the message
pub.publish(person)
```

Services in ROS allow nodes to communicate using a request/response model. This is useful when you need a node to perform an action and wait for the result before continuing.

To define a service, you create a srv file in your package's srv folder. Let's create a AddTwoInts.srv:

```
# AddTwoInts.srv
int32 A
int32 B
---
int32 Sum
```

To generate Python classes for this service, use the following command:

```
rosmsg gensrv --py AddTwoInts.srv add_two_ints.py
```

Here's how you can create a server and client using this service:

Server (add_two_ints_server.py):

```python
from add_two_ints_srv import AddTwoInts, AddTwoIntsRequest, AddTwoIntsResponse


def handle_add_two_ints(req):
    result = req.A + req.B
    return AddTwoIntsResponse(result)


if __name__ == "__main__":
    rospy.init_node('add_two_ints_server')
    srv = rospy.Service('add_two_ints', AddTwoInts, handle_add_two_ints)
    rospy.spin()
```

Client (add_two_ints_client.py):

```
from add_two_ints_srv import AddTwoInts, AddTwoIntsRequest

def add_two_ints_client():
    rospy.wait_for_service('add_two_ints')
    try:
        add_two_ints = rospy.ServiceProxy('add_two_ints', AddTwoInts)
        resp1 = add_two_ints(5, 3)
        print "Sum: %d" % resp1.sum

        resp2 = add_two_ints(7, -2)
        print "Sum: %d" % resp2.sum
    except rospy.ServiceException, e:
        print "Service call failed: %s" % e

if __name__ == "__main__":
    rospy.init_node('add_two_ints_client')
    add_two_ints_client()
```

You've already seen an example of implementing a request/response model with ROS services in the previous section. Here's another example using a custom message:

Server (person_finder_server.py):

```
from Person.msg import Person, PersonArray
import random

people_db = [
    Person(first_name="John", last_name="Doe", age=30),
    Person(first_name="Jane", last_name="Smith", age=25)
]
```

```python
def find_person(req):
    for person in people_db:
        if person.first_name == req.first_name and person.last_name == req.last_name:
            return PersonArray([person])
    return PersonArray([])


if __name__ == "__main__":
    rospy.init_node('person_finder_server')
    srv = rospy.Service('find_person', find_person)
    rospy.spin()
```

Client (person_finder_client.py):

```python
from Person.msg import Person, PersonArray


def find_person_client(first_name, last_name):
    rospy.wait_for_service('find_person')
    try:
        find_person = rospy.ServiceProxy('find_person', find_person)
        req = Person(first_name=first_name, last_name=last_name)
        resp = find_person(req)
        print "Found person:"
        for person in resp.people:
            print "%s %s (%d)" % (person.first_name, person.last_name, person.age)
    except rospy.ServiceException, e:
        print "Service call failed: %s" % e


if __name__ == "__main__":
    rospy.init_node('person_finder_client')
    find_person_client("John", "Doe")
```

Here's a practical example where we use services to control a robot arm:

Server (robot_arm_server.py):

```python
from robot_arm_srv import RobotArmCommand, RobotArmCommandRequest
import random


class RobotArm:
    def __init__(self):
        self.position = 0.0

    def move(self, delta):
        self.position += delta
        if self.position > 180.0:
            self.position -= 360.0
        elif self.position < -180.0:
            self.position += 360.0


def handle_robot_arm_command(req):
    arm.move(req.delta)
    return RobotArmCommandResponse(arm.position)


if __name__ == "__main__":
    rospy.init_node('robot_arm_server')
    arm = RobotArm()
    srv = rospy.Service('robot_arm_command', RobotArmCommand,
handle_robot_arm_command)
    rospy.spin()
```

Client (robot_arm_client.py):

```python
from robot_arm_srv import RobotArmCommand

def control_robot_arm(delta):
    rospy.wait_for_service('robot_arm_command')
    try:
        robot_arm_command = rospy.ServiceProxy('robot_arm_command',
RobotArmCommand)
        resp = robot_arm_command(delta)
        print "Robot arm position: %.2f" % resp.position
    except rospy.ServiceException, e:
        print "Service call failed: %s" % e

if __name__ == "__main__":
    rospy.init_node('robot_arm_client')
    control_robot_arm(30.0)
```

In this example, the client sends a command to the robot arm server with the desired movement delta. The server moves the robot arm accordingly and returns its current position. This way, the client doesn't need to worry about keeping track of the robot arm's state.

Chapter 5: ROS Parameter Server

In this chapter, we will explore the ROS (Robot Operating System) parameter server and how to interact with it using Python. The ROS parameter server is a centralized storage system for parameters used throughout a ROS application. It allows users to retrieve and modify these parameters dynamically at runtime.

The rospy package provides functionalities to access the ROS parameter server from Python. Here's how you can read, write, and use parameters:

```python
import rospy

# Check if a parameter exists
if not rospy.has_param('robot_name'):
    # Set a parameter
    rospy.set_param('robot_name', 'ExampleBot')

# Get the value of a parameter
robot_name = rospy.get_param('robot_name')
print(f"Robot name: {robot_name}")

# Update the value of a parameter
rospy.set_param('robot_name', 'NewExampleBot')
```

You can set parameters using rospy.set_param() and retrieve them using rospy.get_param(). Here's an example:

```python
import rospy

def callback():
```

```python
    # Get the current count value
    count = rospy.get_param('count')

    # Update the count value
    new_count = count + 1
    rospy.set_param('count', new_count)

    print(f"Updated count: {new_count}")

if __name__ == '__main__':
    # Initialize ROS node
    rospy.init_node('param_server_example')

    # Set initial count parameter
    rospy.set_param('count', 0)

    # Create a timer to call the callback function every second
    timer = rospy.Timer(rospy.Duration.from_sec(1), callback)

    # Spin to keep the node running
    rospy.spin()
```

In this example, a ROS node is created that increments and prints a count parameter every second.

Loading Parameters from YAML Files

ROS parameters can be defined in YAML files and then loaded into the parameter server. Here's how you can create a YAML file named robot_params.yaml:

```yaml
# robot_params.yaml
robot_name: ExampleBot
robot_radius: 0.5
```

You can load these parameters into the ROS parameter server using:

```python
import rospy


def load_robot_params():
    # Load parameters from YAML file
    rospy.loginfo('Loading robot params')
    rospy.init_node('load_params', anonymous=True)
    rospy.init_param_from_file('robot_params.yaml')


if __name__ == '__main__':
    load_robot_params()
```

Let's create a ROS node that uses the rospack tool to find the location of an example package, stores it as a parameter, and then retrieves it:

```python
import rospy
import os
import rospkg


def manage_params():
    # Get the location of an example package using rospack
    rp = rospkg.RosPack()
    example_pkg_path = rp.get_path('example_package')

    # Store the path as a ROS parameter
    rospy.set_param('/example_pkg_path', example_pkg_path)

    print(f"Stored example package path: {example_pkg_path}")

    # Retrieve the stored path from the ROS parameter server
```

```python
    retrieved_path = rospy.get_param('/example_pkg_path')
    print(f"Retrieved example package path: {retrieved_path}")


if __name__ == '__main__':
    rospy.init_node('manage_params_example', anonymous=True)
    manage_params()
```

This example demonstrates how to use the ROS parameter server to store and retrieve data dynamically at runtime.

Chapter 6: ROS Packages and Build System

In this chapter, we delve into the intricacies of ROS packages and its build system, focusing on Python-based packages. We'll explore understanding package structure, creating and managing Python-based packages, modifying package.xml for Python dependencies, using catkin_make for compiling mixed-language packages, and best practices for Python-centric ROS development.

ROS packages serve as the fundamental building blocks of ROS systems. They are organized directories that contain code, data, and other assets related to a specific functionality or module within your robot software stack. Here's an overview of the typical ROS package structure:

```
<package_name>/
├── CMakeLists.txt
├── package.xml
├── src/
│   ├── <python_script>.py
│   └── ...
└── ...
```

- CMakeLists.txt: This file is used by ROS's build system, Catkin. It contains rules for compiling and linking source files within the package.
- package.xml: This file provides metadata about the package, such as its dependencies, maintained by tools like roscreate-pkg.
- src/: This directory contains the main source code for the package, including Python scripts.

To create a new Python-based ROS package, use the following command:

```
catkin_create_pkg <package_name> rospy std_msgs
```

This creates a new package named <package_name> with dependencies on rospy (ROS's Python API) and std_msgs. Navigate to your workspace's src/ directory and you'll find the newly created package structure.

Modifying package.xml for Python Dependencies

The package.xml file is crucial for declaring dependencies of a ROS package. For Python-based packages, you typically declare dependencies on ROS-related Python packages like rospy, genpy, or custom message types via the <build_depend>, <run_depend>, and <test_depend> tags.

Here's an example of modifying package.xml to add a dependency on a custom message type:

```xml
<package>
  <name>my_package</name>
  <version>0.1.0</version>
  <description>The my_package package</description>

  <!-- ... existing dependencies ... -->

  <!-- Add this section for custom message types -->
  <build_depend>message_generation</build_depend>
  <run_depend>message_runtime</run_depend>

  <!-- List your messages here -->
  <message_deps>my_msg</message_deps>

  <!-- ... rest of the file ... -->
</package>
```

After modifying package.xml, you need to re-run catkin_make to generate the necessary files for building and using these dependencies.

Using catkin_make for Compiling Mixed-language Packages

ROS packages can contain both C++ and Python code. When building such mixed-language packages, use catkin_make:

```
cd ~/catkin_ws # Navigate to your Catkin workspace
source devel/setup.bash # Source the setup file generated by Catkin
catkin_make # Build your ROS packages
```

After successful compilation, you'll find the binary executables in the devel/lib directory of your Catkin workspace.

Best Practices for Python-centric ROS Development

Here are some best practices to follow when developing ROS packages using Python:

1. **Use clear and descriptive names** for your packages, modules, and functions.
2. **Keep code modular** by separating functionality into different modules or classes.
3. **Follow Python's PEP 8 style guide** for writing clean, readable code.
4. **Use version control** systems like Git to manage changes and collaborate with others.
5. **Write tests** for your code using tools like pytest and unittest.
6. **Document your code** using inline comments and docstrings to explain functionality and usage.
7. **Keep dependencies minimal** by only listing those necessary for your package's functionality.
8. **Use environment variables** like ROS_PACKAGE_PATH and PYTHONPATH to manage ROS packages and Python paths.
9. **Avoid hard-coding values** where possible; use parameters or configuration files instead.

By following these best practices, you'll create maintainable, extensible, and reusable ROS packages using Python.

Chapter 7: ROS Launch Files

ROS (Robot Operating System) provides a powerful mechanism to manage and automate complex robot systems through launch files. Launch files are XML-based configuration files that allow you to specify the nodes, publishers, subscribers, services, parameters, and other elements required for your robot application. In this chapter, we will explore how to write launch files for Python nodes in ROS.

Launch files enable you to encapsulate all the necessary information to run a ROS system, making it easier to manage and reuse across different platforms or environments. They are loaded using the roslaunch command-line tool provided by ROS.

Here's an example of what a simple launch file looks like:

```
<launch>
  <node pkg="turtle_tf" type="turtle_tf_broadcaster.py" name="turtle_tf_broadcaster"/>
</launch>
```

In this example, the launch file contains a single node that publishes a TF (TurtleBot) transformation between the 'world' and 'turtle1' frames. We will cover more details about these elements later in this chapter.

To write launch files for your custom Python nodes, follow these steps:

1. Create an XML file with a .launch extension (e.g., my_node.launch).

2. Enclose the contents of the file within <launch> and </launch> tags.

3. Define the required elements for your node(s) using appropriate ROS tags.

Here's an example launch file for our custom Python node, talker.py:

```
<launch>
  <node pkg="my_package" type="talker.py" name="talker_node"/>
</launch>
```

In this example:

- <node> is the ROS tag used to define a node.
- pkg refers to the package where your node resides (in this case, my_package).
- type specifies the executable file for your node (here, talker.py).
- name assigns a unique name to the node within the ROS system.

To run your launch file, navigate to its location and execute the following command:

roslaunch my_package my_node.launch

This will load your launch file and spawn the specified nodes in the ROS system.

Passing Arguments to Launch Files

Launch files allow you to pass arguments to your nodes using the <arg> tag. These arguments can then be accessed within your Python node using rospy.get_param('name').

Here's an example of a launch file that passes an argument:

```
<launch>
  <arg name="my_arg" default="default_value"/>
  <node pkg="my_package" type="talker.py" name="talker_node">
    <param name="talker_topic" value="$(arg my_arg)"/>
  </node>
</launch>
```

In this example, the launch file defines an argument named my_arg with a default value of "default_value". The <param> tag assigns the value of my_arg to the talker_topic parameter for the talker_node.

Within your Python node (talker.py), you can access this argument using:

```python
import rospy

def talker():
    # Access the argument passed from the launch file
    topic = rospy.get_param('talker_topic')
    ...

if __name__ == '__main__':
    rospy.init_node('talker_node', anonymous=True)
    talker()
```

Launch files are particularly useful when managing complex robot systems with multiple nodes, publishers, subscribers, services, and other ROS elements. Here's an example involving a simple robotic arm application:

Suppose you have the following nodes in your robotic_arm package:

1. controller.py: A node that controls the robotic arm based on joint states and commands.

2. gripper_node.py: A node that publishes gripper status (open or closed) based on button presses.

3. joint_state_publisher.py: A node that publishes the current joint states of the robotic arm.

To create a launch file for this system, follow these steps:

1. Create a new XML file named robotic_arm.launch in your package's launch folder.

2. Define the required nodes and their parameters:

```xml
<launch>
  <node pkg="robotic_arm" type="joint_state_publisher.py"
```

```xml
name="joint_state_publisher"/>
  <node pkg="robotic_arm" type="controller.py" name="controller_node">
    <param name="joint_names" value="joint1 joint2 joint3"/>
    <param name="gripper_topic" value="/gripper_status"/>
  </node>
  <node pkg="robotic_arm" type="gripper_node.py" name="gripper_node"/>

  <!-- Include the gazebo model and simulation -->
  <include file="$(find robotic_arm_gazebo)/launch/empty_world.launch"/>

</launch>
```

In this example:

- We include three nodes: joint_state_publisher, controller, and gripper.
- The controller_node takes two parameters: joint_names (a list of joint names) and gripper_topic (the topic on which gripper status is published).
- We also include a gazebo model using the <include> tag.

With this launch file, you can easily start your robotic arm application by running:

```
roslaunch robotic_arm robotic_arm.launch
```

This will spawn all the required nodes and load the gazebo simulation. You can now interact with your robotic arm using ROS topics and services.

Conclusion

In this chapter, we explored the power of ROS launch files for managing complex robot systems. We learned how to write launch files for Python nodes, pass arguments to them, and use practical examples to create launch files for managing multiple nodes in a robotic application.

By utilizing launch files, you can encapsulate your ROS system's configuration, making it easier to manage, reuse, and share with others.

Chapter 8: Transformations with tf and tf2

In this chapter, we will explore the tf (transforms) library in ROS, which is essential for managing coordinate frames. We'll cover both the original tf package and its successor, tf2.

Introduction to tf and tf2 in Python

The tf package provides functionalities to manage transforms between different coordinate frames. It uses a graph structure where each node represents a coordinate frame, and edges represent transformations between them.

The newer tf2 library is designed to improve upon the original tf by providing more efficient and flexible transformations. It introduces concepts like static and dynamic broadcasters, as well as improved error handling.

Here's how you can import them in Python:

```python
import tf  # Original tf package
import tf2_ros  # tf2 library with better functionalities
```

Broadcasting and listening to transforms with rospy

To work with transforms, we need to understand broadcasting and listening to transform data. We'll use the rospy library for this.

Broadcasting a transform

First, let's see how to broadcast a static transform using ROS's tf2_ros.StaticTransformBroadcaster:

```python
import tf2_ros
import geometry_msgs.msg


def broadcast_static_transform():
    br = tf2_ros.StaticTransformBroadcaster()
```

```python
    t = geometry_msgs.msg.TransformStamped()

    t.header.stamp = rospy.Time.now()
    t.header.frame_id = "frame_A"
    t.child_frame_id = "frame_B"

    t.transform.translation.x = 1.0
    t.transform.translation.y = 2.0
    t.transform.translation.z = 3.0

    t.transform.rotation =
geometry_msgs.msg.Quaternion(*tf.transformations.quaternion_from_euler(0, 0, 1.57))
# rotate around Z by pi/2

    br.sendTransform(t)

if __name__ == "__main__":
    rospy.init_node('static_tf_broadcaster')
    broadcast_static_transform()
    rospy.spin()
```

Listening to transforms

Now let's see how to listen for transform data using ROS's tf2_ros.Buffer:

```python
import tf2_ros
from geometry_msgs.msg import TransformStamped

def listen_to_transforms():
    buffer = tf2_ros.Buffer()
    listener = tf2_ros.TransformListener(buffer)

    while not rospy.is_shutdown():
```

```python
    try:
        trans = buffer.lookup_transform('frame_B', 'frame_A', rospy.Time(0))
        print("Transform from frame_B to frame_A:\n{}".format(trans))
        rospy.sleep(1.0)
    except (tf2_ros.LookupException, tf2_ros ConnectivityException,
tf2_ros.ExtrapolationException) as e:
        print(e)


if __name__ == "__main__":
    rospy.init_node('transform_listener')
    listen_to_transforms()
```

Let's explore some practical examples using tf and tf2.

Example 1: Publishing a static transform between two frames

In this example, we'll publish a static transform between two coordinate frames (frame_A and frame_B).

```python
import rospy
from geometry_msgs.msg import TransformStamped


def publish_static_transform():
    pub = rospy.Publisher('/static_transform', TransformStamped, queue_size=1)

    rate = rospy.Rate(10) # 10 Hz
    while not rospy.is_shutdown():
        t = TransformStamped()
        t.header.stamp = rospy.Time.now()
        t.header.frame_id = "frame_A"
        t.child_frame_id = "frame_B"
```

```
    t.transform.translation.x = 1.0
    t.transform.rotation.w = 1.0 # No rotation


    pub.publish(t)
    rate.sleep()


if __name__ == "__main__":
    rospy.init_node('static_transform_publisher')
    publish_static_transform()
```

Example 2: Listening to dynamic transforms and visualizing them in rviz

In this example, we'll listen to dynamic transform data from a
tf2_ros.StaticTransformBroadcaster node (like the one in the broadcasting section), and
visualize it in rviz.

1. First, launch the static_tf_broadcaster.py node.
2. Create a .rviz file with the following settings:
    -   Add a TF display with topic /tf_static.
    -   Set the fixed frame to your desired coordinate frame (e.g., "map").
3. Run rviz and open your .rviz file.

You should now see the transform between frame_A and frame_B.

Visualizing transforms in rviz

As seen in the previous example, you can visualize transforms in rviz using the TF
display. This allows you to better understand and debug transformations between
coordinate frames.

Chapter 9: Sensor Integration

In this chapter, we will explore how to interface with various sensors such as cameras, LiDARs, and Inertial Measurement Units (IMUs) in ROS using Python. We'll cover reading and processing sensor data, using sensor message types in Python nodes, and provide practical examples of real-time sensor data handling.

Interfacing Sensors

ROS provides a standardized way to interface with sensors by defining sensor messages and providing drivers for popular sensors. Here's how you can integrate common sensors:

Cameras

To use cameras in ROS, you'll typically need a driver that publishes images over the sensor_msgs/Image topic. For example, if you're using a USB camera like the Logitech C920, you can use the webcam_image_producer node provided by the image_transport package:

```python
import rospy
from sensor_msgs.msg import Image


def image_callback(msg):
    # Process image here
    pass


def main():
    rospy.init_node('camera_listener')
    rospy.Subscriber('/webcam/image_raw', Image, image_callback)
    rospy.spin()


if __name__ == '__main__':
    main()
```

LiDARs

LiDAR sensors publish point cloud data over the sensor_msgs/PointCloud2 topic.
Here's how you can listen to a LiDAR sensor using the velodyne_pointcloud package:

```python
import rospy
from sensor_msgs.msg import PointCloud2


def pcl_callback(msg):
    # Process point cloud here
    pass


def main():
    rospy.init_node('lidar_listener')
    rospy.Subscriber('/velodyne/point_cloud', PointCloud2, pcl_callback)
    rospy.spin()


if __name__ == '__main__':
    main()
```

IMUs

IMU sensors publish orientation and angular velocity data over the sensor_msgs/Imu
topic. Here's how you can listen to an IMU sensor:

```python
import rospy
from sensor_msgs.msg import Imu


def imu_callback(msg):
    # Process IMU data here
    pass


def main():
    rospy.init_node('imu_listener')
```

```python
    rospy.Subscriber('/imu/data', Imu, imu_callback)
    rospy.spin()


if __name__ == '__main__':
    main()
```

Reading and Processing Sensor Data in Python

Once you have subscribed to a sensor topic, you can process the data in various ways. Here are some examples:

Cameras: Image Processing

You can use OpenCV or PIL to process images from ROS topics:

```python
import rospy
from sensor_msgs.msg import Image
import cv2
from cv_bridge import CvBridge


def image_callback(msg):
    # Convert ROS image message to OpenCV format
    bridge = CvBridge()
    cv_image = bridge.imgmsg_to_cv2(msg, 'bgr8')

    # Process image using OpenCV functions
    gray_image = cv2.cvtColor(cv_image, cv2.COLOR_BGR2GRAY)


def main():
    rospy.init_node('camera_processor')
    rospy.Subscriber('/webcam/image_raw', Image, image_callback)
    rospy.spin()
```

```python
if __name__ == '__main__':
    main()
```

LiDARs: Point Cloud Processing

You can use the pcl library to process point cloud data:

```python
import rospy
from sensor_msgs.msg import PointCloud2
import pcl


def pcl_callback(msg):
    # Convert ROS point cloud message to PCL format
    pcl_msg = pcl.PCLPointCloud2()
    pcl_msg.from_array(msg.data)
    pcl_msg.deserialize()

    # Process point cloud using PCL functions
    passfilter = pcl_filters.PassThroughFilter()
    passfilter.setFilterFieldName("z")
    passfilter.setFilterLimits(0.3, 1.5)


def main():
    rospy.init_node('lidar_processor')
    rospy.Subscriber('/velodyne/point_cloud', PointCloud2, pcl_callback)
    rospy.spin()


if __name__ == '__main__':
    main()
```

IMUs: Data Filtering

You can use the scipy library to filter IMU data:

```python
import rospy
from sensor_msgs.msg import Imu
import numpy as np
from scipy.signal import butter, lfilter


def imu_callback(msg):
    # Define low-pass Butterworth filter parameters
    fs = 50.0      # sampling rate, Hz
    cutoff = 5.0   # desired cutoff frequency, Hz

    nyq = 0.5 * fs
    normal_cutoff = cutoff / nyq
    b, a = butter(N=4, Wn=normal_cutoff, btype='low', analog=False)

    # Filter angular velocity data using the defined filter coefficients
    msg.angular_velocity.x = lfilter(b, a, np.array([msg.angular_velocity.x]))
    msg.angular_velocity.y = lfilter(b, a, np.array([msg.angular_velocity.y]))
    msg.angular_velocity.z = lfilter(b, a, np.array([msg.angular_velocity.z]))

def main():
    rospy.init_node('imu_filter')
    rospy.Subscriber('/imu/data', Imu, imu_callback)
    rospy.spin()

if __name__ == '__main__':
    main()
```

When publishing sensor data from a custom node, you should use the appropriate ROS message type. Here's how you can publish sensor messages:

Cameras: Publishing Images

```python
import rospy
from sensor_msgs.msg import Image
import cv2
from cv_bridge import CvBridge


def main():
    pub = rospy.Publisher('/custom/image', Image, queue_size=1)
    bridge = CvBridge()
    rospy.init_node('camera_publisher')
    rate = rospy.Rate(5) # 5 Hz

    while not rospy.is_shutdown():
        # Capture image using OpenCV
        ret, frame = cv2.VideoCapture(0).read()

        if ret:
            msg = bridge.cv2_to_imgmsg(frame, 'bgr8')
            pub.publish(msg)

        rate.sleep()

if __name__ == '__main__':
    main()
```

LiDARs: Publishing Point Cloud Data

```python
import rospy
from sensor_msgs.msg import PointCloud2
import pcl


def main():
    pub = rospy.Publisher('/custom/point_cloud', PointCloud2, queue_size=1)
```

```python
    rospy.init_node('lidar_publisher')
    rate = rospy.Rate(5) # 5 Hz

    while not rospy.is_shutdown():
        # Generate point cloud using PCL
        pcl_msg = pcl.PCLPointCloud2()
        pcl_msg.from_file('sample.pcd')

        msg = PointCloud2()
        msg.header.stamp = rospy.Time.now()
        msg.header.frame_id = 'custom_frame'
        msg.data = pcl_msg.to_array()
        msg.width = pcl_msg.width
        msg.height = pcl_msg.height
        msg.fields = pcl_msg.fields
        msg.is_dense = pcl_msg.is_dense
        msg.is_bigendian = False

        pub.publish(msg)

        rate.sleep()

if __name__ == '__main__':
    main()
```

IMUs: Publishing Orientation and Angular Velocity Data

```python
import rospy
from sensor_msgs.msg import Imu
import random

def main():
    pub = rospy.Publisher('/custom/imu', Imu, queue_size=1)
```

```python
rospy.init_node('imu_publisher')
rate = rospy.Rate(50) # 50 Hz

while not rospy.is_shutdown():
    msg = Imu()
    msg.header.stamp = rospy.Time.now()
    msg.header.frame_id = 'custom_frame'
    msg.orientation.x = random.random() - 0.5
    msg.orientation.y = random.random() - 0.5
    msg.orientation.z = random.random() - 0.5
    msg.orientation.w = random.random()
    msg.angular_velocity.x = random.gauss(0, 1)
    msg.angular_velocity.y = random.gauss(0, 1)
    msg.angular_velocity.z = random.gauss(0, 1)

    pub.publish(msg)

    rate.sleep()

if __name__ == '__main__':
    main()
```

Practical Examples of Real-time Sensor Data Handling

Here's a practical example that combines real-time sensor data processing and publishing:

```python
import rospy
from sensor_msgs.msg import Image, PointCloud2
import cv2
from cv_bridge import CvBridge
import pcl
```

```python
def image_callback(msg):
    global bridge, pub_point_cloud
    # Convert ROS image message to OpenCV format
    cv_image = bridge.imgmsg_to_cv2(msg, 'bgr8')

    # Process image using OpenCV functions and extract edges
    gray_image = cv2.cvtColor(cv_image, cv2.COLOR_BGR2GRAY)
    edges = cv2.Canny(gray_image, 50, 150)

    # Publish point cloud data generated from image edges
    pcl_msg = pcl.PCLPointCloud2()
    pcl_msg.from_array(edges.tostring())
    msg_point_cloud = PointCloud2()
    msg_point_cloud.header.stamp = rospy.Time.now()
    msg_point_cloud.header.frame_id = 'custom_frame'
    msg_point_cloud.data = pcl_msg.to_array()
    msg_point_cloud.width = edges.shape[1]
    msg_point_cloud.height = edges.shape[0]
    msg_point_cloud.fields = [{'name': 'x', 'offset': 0, 'datatype': PointCloud2.FLOAT32, 'count': 1},
                    {'name': 'y', 'offset': 4, 'datatype': PointCloud2.FLOAT32, 'count': 1}]
    msg_point_cloud.is_dense = False
    msg_point_cloud.is_bigendian = False

    pub_point_cloud.publish(msg_point_cloud)

def main():
    global bridge, pub_point_cloud
    rospy.init_node('sensor_processor')
    rate = rospy.Rate(5) # 5 Hz
```

```python
    bridge = CvBridge()
    pub_point_cloud = rospy.Publisher('/custom/point_cloud_from_image', PointCloud2,
queue_size=1)
    rospy.Subscriber('/webcam/image_raw', Image, image_callback)

    while not rospy.is_shutdown():
        rate.sleep()


if __name__ == '__main__':
    main()
```

In this example, we subscribe to a camera topic, process the image using OpenCV to extract edges, and publish the resulting point cloud data. This demonstrates how you can combine real-time sensor data processing with publishing in ROS Python nodes.

That concludes our overview of sensor integration in ROS using Python.

Chapter 10: Actuators and Robot Control

In this chapter, we will delve into the world of robot actuation and control using ROS (Robot Operating System) with Python. We will cover four main topics: writing Python nodes for motor and actuator control, using ROS control with Python, practical examples of robotic arm and wheel control, and integrating custom hardware drivers.

To control motors or actuators in ROS, we first need to create a node that publishes commands to the appropriate topics. Here's a simple example of a Python node that publishes linear velocities to a topic named /cmd_vel:

```python
#!/usr/bin/env python
import rospy
from geometry_msgs.msg import Twist

def move():
    pub = rospy.Publisher('/cmd_vel', Twist, queue_size=10)
    rospy.init_node('actuator_node', anonymous=True)

    rate = rospy.Rate(10) # 10hz
    twist = Twist()

    while not rospy.is_shutdown():
        twist.linear.x = 0.5 # Set linear velocity to 0.5 m/s
        pub.publish(twist)
        rate.sleep()

if __name__ == '__main__':
    try:
        move()
```

```
except rospy.ROSInterruptException:
    pass
```

In this example, we first import the necessary ROS libraries and define a function move() that initializes a node named actuator_node. We then create a publisher that publishes to the /cmd_vel topic with a message type of Twist.

Within the while loop, we set the linear velocity (linear.x) to 0.5 m/s and publish this command using pub.publish(twist). The rate is set to 10 Hz using rospy.Rate(10), meaning that the node will publish commands at a frequency of 10 Hz.

To run this node, save it as actuator_node.py and ensure you have given it executable permissions (chmod +x actuator_node.py). Then, run it with the following command:

```
rosrun your_package_name actuator_node.py
```

Using ROS Control with Python

ROS Control is a collection of packages that provide support for robot control in ROS. It includes tools for commanding robots via topics and services, and for controlling robots using joint controllers.

To use ROS Control with Python, we'll first need to create a controller_manager.launch file to load the necessary controllers. Here's an example of a simple joint trajectory controller for a two-joint robotic arm:

```xml
<launch>
  <arg name="arm_name" default="my_robot_arm"/>

  <!-- Load robot model -->
  <include file="$(find my_package_name)/urdf/arm_model.xacro"/>
  <node pkg="robot_state_publisher" type="robot_state_publisher"
      name="robot_state_publisher">
    <param name="publish_frequency" value="10"/>
    <param name="tf_prefix" value="base_link"/>
```

```xml
    </node>

    <!-- Load controllers -->
    <node pkg="controller_manager" type="spawner.py" name="controller_spawner"
        args="joint_state_controller joint_traj_controller
            -j arm_name/joint_1
            -j arm_name/joint_2"/>

</launch>
```

In this example, we first load the robot model using xacro and publish its state using robot_state_publisher. We then spawn two controllers: joint_state_controller to publish joint states, and joint_traj_controller to control the joints.

Next, let's create a Python node that sends a trajectory to the robotic arm using ROS Control:

```python
#!/usr/bin/env python
import rospy
from trajectory_msgs.msg import JointTrajectory
from trajectory_msgs.msg import JointTrajectoryPoint

def send_trajectory():
    pub = rospy.Publisher('/arm_name/joint_traj_controller/command', JointTrajectory,
queue_size=10)
    rospy.init_node('trajectory_node', anonymous=True)

    rate = rospy.Rate(1) # 1hz
    trajectory = JointTrajectory()

    while not rospy.is_shutdown():
        point = JointTrajectoryPoint()
        point.positions = [0.5, -0.5] # Set joint positions
```

```
        trajectory.points.append(point)


        pub.publish(trajectory)
        rate.sleep()


if __name__ == '__main__':
    try:
        send_trajectory()
    except rospy.ROSInterruptException:
        pass
```

In this example, we publish a JointTrajectory message to the
/arm_name/joint_traj_controller/command topic. Within the while loop, we create a new
JointTrajectoryPoint with desired joint positions and append it to the trajectory. We then
publish the trajectory using pub.publish(trajectory).

Practical Examples of Robotic Arm and Wheel Control

Now that we have covered the basics of actuator control with ROS and Python, let's
look at some practical examples.

Robotic Arm Control

To control a robotic arm, we'll use the same approach as in the previous section. First,
make sure you have loaded the appropriate controllers using a
controller_manager.launch file. Then, create a Python node that publishes joint
trajectories to control the robotic arm:

```
#!/usr/bin/env python
import rospy
from trajectory_msgs.msg import JointTrajectory
from trajectory_msgs.msg import JointTrajectoryPoint


def move_arm():
```

```python
    pub = rospy.Publisher('/arm_name/joint_traj_controller/command', JointTrajectory,
queue_size=10)
    rospy.init_node('arm_control_node', anonymous=True)

    rate = rospy.Rate(1) # 1hz
    trajectory = JointTrajectory()

    while not rospy.is_shutdown():
        point = JointTrajectoryPoint()
        point.positions = [0.5, -0.5] # Set joint positions
        trajectory.points.append(point)

        pub.publish(trajectory)
        rate.sleep()

if __name__ == '__main__':
    try:
        move_arm()
    except rospy.ROSInterruptException:
        pass
```

In this example, replace /arm_name with the name of your robotic arm's namespace. You can also modify the joint positions to suit your desired movement.

Wheel Control

To control wheels using ROS and Python, we'll publish velocities to the appropriate topic(s). Here's an example that publishes linear and angular velocities to control a differential drive robot:

```python
#!/usr/bin/env python
import rospy
from geometry_msgs.msg import Twist
```

```python
def drive_wheels():
    pub = rospy.Publisher('/cmd_vel', Twist, queue_size=10)
    rospy.init_node('wheel_control_node', anonymous=True)

    rate = rospy.Rate(10) # 10hz
    twist = Twist()

    while not rospy.is_shutdown():
        twist.linear.x = 0.5 # Set linear velocity to 0.5 m/s
        twist.angular.z = 0.2 # Set angular velocity to 0.2 rad/s
        pub.publish(twist)
        rate.sleep()

if __name__ == '__main__':
    try:
        drive_wheels()
    except rospy.ROSInterruptException:
        pass
```

In this example, we publish velocities to the /cmd_vel topic using a Twist message. Within the while loop, set the desired linear (linear.x) and angular (angular.z) velocities accordingly.

Integrating Custom Hardware Drivers

Integrating custom hardware drivers involves creating new ROS nodes that interact with your custom hardware directly or through device drivers. Here's an example of how to integrate a custom motor driver using Python:

1. First, make sure you have created a device driver for your custom hardware that allows you to control it programmatically.

2. Create a new Python node that interacts with the device driver and publishes commands to ROS topics.

Here's an example of a Python node that controls a custom motor driver and publishes its status to a ROS topic:

```python
#!/usr/bin/env python
import rospy
from std_msgs.msg import Float32


class MotorDriverNode:
    def __init__(self):
        self.pub = rospy.Publisher('/motor_status', Float32, queue_size=10)
        rospy.init_node('motor_driver_node')

        # Initialize custom hardware driver
        self.driver = CustomMotorDriver()


    def run(self):
        rate = rospy.Rate(10) # 10hz

        while not rospy.is_shutdown():
            # Set motor speed using your device driver's API
            self.driver.set_speed(0.5)

            # Publish motor status (e.g., current)
            msg = Float32()
            msg.data = self.driver.get_current()
            self.pub.publish(msg)

            rate.sleep()
```

```python
if __name__ == '__main__':
    try:
        node = MotorDriverNode()
        node.run()
    except rospy.ROSInterruptException:
        pass
```

In this example, we define a MotorDriverNode class that initializes the custom hardware driver and runs the main loop. Within the while loop, we set the motor speed using the device driver's API and publish its current status to the /motor_status topic.

To run this node, save it as motor_driver_node.py, make it executable (chmod +x motor_driver_node.py), and run it with the following command:

rosrun your_package_name motor_driver_node.py

In conclusion, this chapter has covered the fundamentals of actuator control using ROS and Python, including writing Python nodes for motor and actuator control, using ROS Control with Python, practical examples of robotic arm and wheel control, and integrating custom hardware drivers. With these concepts in hand, you are now ready to build more advanced robotics applications using ROS and Python.

Chapter 11: Working with RViz and Gazebo

This chapter introduces you to working with **RViz** for visualization and **Gazebo** for simulation in ROS (Robot Operating System). We'll cover simulating robots in Gazebo, writing Python plugins for Gazebo, using Python for visualization in RViz, and provide practical examples of debugging and simulation.

Simulating Robots in Gazebo

Gazebo is a popular robotics simulator used with ROS. It allows you to simulate complex robotic systems in various environments. Here's how you can simulate a robot in Gazebo:

1. **Launch Gazebo world:**

```python
import rospy
from gazebo_msgs.srv import DeleteModel, SpawnModel


def spawn_robot():
    # Initialize node
    rospy.init_node('spawn_robot')


    # Load robot model from URDF
    with open("robot_model.urdf", "r") as f:
        robot_model = f.read()


    # Spawn robot in Gazebo
    spawn_srv = rospy.ServiceProxy('/gazebo/spawn_ury_model', SpawnModel)
    spawn_srv(model_name='my_robot',
        robot_xml=robot_model,
        initial_pose={'position': [0, 0, 1], 'orientation': [0, 0, 0, 1]})
```

```python
if __name__ == '__main__':
    spawn_robot()
```

2. **Publish odometry data:**

```python
import rospy
from nav_msgs.msg import Odometry


def publish_odometry():
    pub = rospy.Publisher('/odom', Odometry, queue_size=5)
    rospy.init_node('publish_odometry')
    rate = rospy.Rate(10)  # 10 Hz

    while not rospy.is_shutdown():
        odom = Odometry()
        odom.header.stamp = rospy.Time.now()
        odom.pose.pose.position.x = ...  # Set x, y, z positions
        pub.publish(odom)
        rate.sleep()


if __name__ == '__main__':
    publish_odometry()
```

Writing Python Plugins for Gazebo

Gazebo supports plugins written in Python. Here's an example of a simple plugin that logs the robot's linear velocity:

```python
import gazebo
from gazebo import msgs


class LogLinearVelocity(gazebo.components.Component):
    def __init__(self):
        super(LogLinearVelocity, self).__init__()
```

```python
        self._vel = None

    def load(self, name, node):
        self._node = node
        self._sub = self._node.Subscriber('/odom', msgs.Odometry)

    def update(self):
        msg = self._sub.Take()
        if msg:
            print(f"Linear velocity: {msg.linear}")
```

To use this plugin:

1. Save it as log_linear_velocity.py.
2. Build the Gazebo plugin using catkin: catkin_make_gazebo_plugins.
3. Load the plugin with your robot model.

```
rosrun gazebo_ros spawn_model -file `rospack find my_package`/urdf/my_robot.urdf -model my_robot -entity my_entity -x 0 -y 0 -z 1.5 -world default.world
rosrun gazebo_ros load_plugin GazeboRosPythonPlugin /path/to/log_linear_velocity.py
```

Using Python for Visualization in RViz

RViz is a powerful tool for visualizing ROS data. You can use it to visualize your robot's pose, sensor data, and more. Here's how you can use RViz with a simple Python script publishing a PoseStamped message:

```python
import rospy
from geometry_msgs.msg import PoseStamped

def publish_pose():
    pub = rospy.Publisher('/robot_pose', PoseStamped, queue_size=5)
    rospy.init_node('publish_pose')
    rate = rospy.Rate(10)  # 10 Hz
```

```python
    while not rospy.is_shutdown():
        pose = PoseStamped()
        pose.header.stamp = rospy.Time.now()
        pose.pose.position.x = ...  # Set x, y, z positions
        pub.publish(pose)
        rate.sleep()


if __name__ == '__main__':
    publish_pose()
```

To visualize this data in RViz:

1. Launch RViz with your desired display configuration.
2. Add a new display for /robot_pose with a PoseStamped message type.

Practical Examples of Debugging and Simulation

Let's consider an example where we want to debug why our robot isn't moving as expected. We can use Gazebo for simulation and RViz for visualization.

1. **Simulate the robot in Gazebo:**

```python
import rospy
from gazebo_msgs.srv import SpawnModel, DeleteModel


def spawn_robot():
    # ... (same as before)


if __name__ == '__main__':
    spawn_robot()
```

2. **Publish odometry data:**

```python
# ... (same as before)
```

3. **Visualize the robot's pose in RViz:**
   - Add a display for /odom with a nav_msgs/msg/Odometry message type.
   - Add a display for the robot model with an rviz_default_display_type_plugins/TurtleBot3Model.

4. **Debugging:** If the robot isn't moving as expected, you can:
   - Check if the /odom topic is publishing data using rostopic echo.
   - Visualize the robot's linear velocity using a plugin (as shown earlier).
   - Inspect the robot's joints and their velocities in RViz.

By following these steps, you should be able to effectively work with RViz and Gazebo for visualization and simulation tasks.

Chapter 12: Debugging and Logging

This chapter focuses on debugging and logging techniques essential for developing robust ROS (Robot Operating System) applications using Python. We'll cover Python logging in ROS, debugging Python nodes with the pdb module, monitoring ROS systems using rqt tools, and best practices for debugging Python-based ROS applications.

Using Python Logging in ROS

ROS provides built-in logging functionality through the rospy library. You can use it to log messages at various levels of severity: DEBUG, INFO, WARN, ERROR, and FATAL. The logs are published on the /rosout topic and can be viewed using tools like rqt_console.

Here's a simple example demonstrating how to use logging in ROS:

```python
import rospy

def talker():
    rospy.init_node('talker', anonymous=True)

    rate = rospy.Rate(1)  # 1 Hz
    while not rospy.is_shutdown():
        rospy.loginfo("Hello, ROS!")
        rate.sleep()

if __name__ == '__main__':
    try:
        talker()
    except rospy.ROSInterruptException:
        pass
```

In this example, the rospy.loginfo() function is used to log an info-level message "Hello, ROS!" at a frequency of 1 Hz.

You can also use Python's built-in logging module for more advanced logging features like formatting and handlers:

```python
import rospy
import logging


def talker():
    rospy.init_node('talker', anonymous=True)

    # Set up custom logger
    logger = logging.getLogger(__name__)
    logger.setLevel(logging.INFO)
    handler = logging.StreamHandler()
    formatter = logging.Formatter('%(asctime)s - %(levelname)s - %(message)s')
    handler.setFormatter(formatter)
    logger.addHandler(handler)

    rate = rospy.Rate(1)  # 1 Hz
    while not rospy.is_shutdown():
        logger.info("Hello, ROS!")
        rate.sleep()


if __name__ == '__main__':
    try:
        talker()
    except rospy.ROSInterruptException:
        pass
```

In this version, we use a custom logger with a timestamp and severity level in the log messages.

The pdb module provides a simple command-line interface for debugging Python programs. Here's how you can use it to debug ROS nodes:

1. Add import pdb; pdb.set_trace() at the desired breakpoint in your node.

```python
import rospy
import pdb


def talker():
    rospy.init_node('talker', anonymous=True)
    rate = rospy.Rate(1)  # 1 Hz


    import pdb; pdb.set_trace()  # Set breakpoint here


    while not rospy.is_shutdown():
        rospy.loginfo("Hello, ROS!")
        rate.sleep()

if __name__ == '__main__':
    try:
        talker()
    except rospy.ROSInterruptException:
        pass
```

2. Run your node with the --ros-args flag -d to enable debugging:

```
rosrun your_package your_node -d
```

3. Once the breakpoint is hit, you'll enter the pdb debugger. You can use various commands like n, s, c, and p to step through the code, inspect variables, etc.

For more information on pdb commands, consult the official Python documentation: https://docs.python.org/3/library/pdb.html

ROS provides several tools for monitoring ROS systems, collectively known as rqt plugins. Some useful plugins for debugging include:

- **rqt_console**: Displays logged messages from topics like /rosout.
- **rqt_graph**: Visualizes the active publishers and subscribers in the system.
- **rqt_gui**: Provides a centralized interface for launching, managing, and monitoring ROS nodes.

To use these tools, simply run them as you would any other ROS node:

```
rosrun rqt_console rqt_console
rosrun rqt_graph rqt_graph
rosrun rqt_gui rqt_gui
```

1. **Be specific**: Clearly state the issue or problem you're trying to solve before starting the debugging process.
2. **Use logging liberally**: Log messages at appropriate levels (INFO, WARN, ERROR) to track the flow of your node and catch unexpected behavior.
3. **Set breakpoints strategically**: Focus on critical sections of your code where things might go wrong.
4. **Inspect variables** using pdb or a debugger like PyCharm. Make sure to check both data types and values.
5. **Use tools wisely**:
   - rqt_console: Monitor log messages for errors and warnings.
   - rqt_graph: Visualize the system's publishers and subscribers to ensure they're connected as expected.
   - rqt_gui: Manage nodes and monitor their status.

6. **Keep it simple**: Avoid unnecessary complexity in your code. Smaller, single-purpose functions are easier to debug than large, monolithic ones.

By following these best practices, you'll be well-equipped to tackle debugging challenges in Python-based ROS applications efficiently.

Chapter 13: Robot Localization and Mapping

In this chapter, we'll explore the crucial aspects of robot localization and mapping using ROS (Robot Operating System) with Python. We'll focus on implementing SLAM (Simultaneous Localization and Mapping), utilizing Python-based ROS packages like gmapping and cartographer, and visualizing mapping outputs in rviz.

Implementing SLAM

SLAM is a fundamental process where a robot builds or updates a map of its environment while simultaneously keeping track of its location within that map. This chapter will guide you through implementing SLAM using ROS packages in Python.

Setting Up the Environment

Before we begin, ensure you have ROS installed on your system and set up properly. For this chapter, we'll be using ROS Noetic Ninjemys (Melodic Morenia or newer). You'll also need to install the necessary ROS packages:

```
sudo apt-get update && sudo apt-get install ros-noetic-gmapping ros-noetic-cartographer
```

Using gmapping

gmapping is a popular ROS package that implements a Rao-Blackwellized particle filter for simultaneous localization and mapping. Here's how you can use it in Python:

1. **Create a launch file**

In your workspace's launch folder, create a new XML file named gmapping.launch:

```xml
<launch>
  <node pkg="gmapping" type="slam_gmapping" name="gMapping">
    <rosparam command="load" file="$(find your_package)/params/gmapping.yaml"/>
  </node>
</launch>
```

Replace 'your_package' with the name of your ROS package.

2.   Configure parameters

Create a YAML file named gmapping.yaml in your workspace's config folder:

```yaml
frequency: 10
maxRange: 4.0
minRange: 0.1
sigma: 0.1
kernelSize: 1
lstep: 0.1
astep: 0.5
iterations: 5
lsigma: 0.1
ogain: 3.0
pmgain: 2.0
kldErr: 0.05
mapUpdateInterval: 1
maxNewLandmarks: 300
```

3.   Run the launch file

In your terminal, run:

```
roscore
roslaunch your_package gmapping.launch
```

Replace 'your_package' with the name of your ROS package.

4.   Publish sensor data

For gmapping to work, you need to publish laser scan messages (sensor_msgs/LaserScan). You can use a Bag file containing laser scan data or publish simulated data using a node like scan_publisher:

```
rosrun your_package scan_publisher.py
```

Replace 'your_package' with the name of your ROS package.

5. Visualize the map

To visualize the output map in rviz, create a new rviz configuration file and add:

- A Map display with topic /map
- A LaserScan display with topic /scan

Now you should see the robot navigating and mapping its environment in real-time.

Using cartographer

cartographer is another powerful ROS package for SLAM, utilizing the Iterative Closest Point (ICP) algorithm. Here's how to use it:

1. Create a launch file

In your workspace's launch folder, create a new XML file named cartographer.launch:

```
<launch>
  <node pkg="cartographer_ros" type="cartographer_node" name="cartographer">
    <rosparam command="load" file="$(find your_package)/params/cartographer.yaml"/>
  </node>
</launch>
```

Replace 'your_package' with the name of your ROS package.

2. Configure parameters

Create a YAML file named cartographer.yaml in your workspace's config folder:

```
resolution: 0.05
publish_robustified_data: true
use_gpu: false
scan_topic: "/scan"
```

map_publish_period: 1
pose_publish_frequency: 1

3. **Run the launch file**

In your terminal, run:

```
roscore
roslaunch your_package cartographer.launch
```

Replace 'your_package' with the name of your ROS package.

4. **Publish sensor data**

Similar to gmapping, you need to publish laser scan messages (sensor_msgs/LaserScan) for cartographer to work. You can use the same methods as described in the previous section.

5. **Visualize the map**

To visualize the output map in rviz, follow the same steps as when using gmapping.

Practical Examples of Real-Time Mapping

Let's explore two practical examples of real-time mapping using Python-based ROS packages.

Example 1: Mapping a Known Environment with gmapping

In this example, we'll use gmapping to map a known environment while simulating laser scan data. Create the following Python script (scan_publisher.py) in your workspace's scripts folder:

```python
#!/usr/bin/env python
import rospy
from sensor_msgs.msg import LaserScan


def scan_callback():
```

```python
    pub = rospy.Publisher('/scan', LaserScan, queue_size=10)
    r = rospy.Rate(10)  # 10 Hz
    while not rospy.is_shutdown():
        msg = LaserScan()
        msg.header.frame_id = 'base_laser_link'
        msg.angle_min = -1.5708
        msg.angle_max = 1.5708
        msg.angle_increment = 0.01745329251
        msg.time_increment = 0.001
        msg.range_min = 0.1
        msg.range_max = 4.0


        # Populate ranges with data from a known environment or sensor readings
        for i in range(96):
            msg.ranges.append(2 + sin(i * msg.angle_increment))


        pub.publish(msg)
        r.sleep()


if __name__ == '__main__':
    rospy.init_node('scan_publisher', anonymous=True)
    scan_callback()
```

Replace 'your_package' with the name of your ROS package, and run:

```
rosrun your_package scan_publisher.py
roslaunch your_package gmapping.launch
```

Now you should see gmapping creating a map of the known environment in rviz.

Example 2: Mapping an Unknown Environment with cartographer

In this example, we'll use cartographer to map an unknown environment while publishing real laser scan data from a TurtleBot:

1. **Set up your TurtleBot**

Make sure you have a functioning TurtleBot with ROS installed and set up properly. For this example, assume you're using a Hokuyo URG-04LX laser scanner connected to the TurtleBot's /scan topic.

2. **Create launch files**

In your workspace's launch folder, create two new XML files named turtlebot.launch and cartographer.launch:

turtlebot.launch:

```
<launch>
  <include file="$(find turtlebot_bringup)/launch/minimal.launch"/>
  <node pkg="your_package" type="scan_publisher.py" name="scan_publisher"/>
</launch>
```

cartographer.launch:

```
<launch>
  <node pkg="cartographer_ros" type="cartographer_node" name="cartographer">
    <rosparam command="load" file="$(find
your_package)/params/cartographer.yaml"/>
  </node>
</launch>
```

Replace 'your_package' with the name of your ROS package.

3. **Run the launch files**

In your terminal, run:

```
roscore
roslaunch your_package turtlebot.launch
roslaunch your_package cartographer.launch
```

Now you should see cartographer creating a map of the unknown environment as the TurtleBot navigates around in rviz.

These examples demonstrate how to use Python-based ROS packages like gmapping and cartographer for real-time mapping. You can adapt these scripts to fit your specific robot hardware and environments.

Visualizing Mapping Outputs in rviz

rviz is a powerful tool for visualizing sensor data, maps, and other information related to ROS nodes. Here's how you can visualize mapping outputs:

1. **Create a new rviz configuration file**

Open rviz, click on File -> Save As, and choose a location for your new configuration file (e.g., mapping.rviz).

2. **Add displays**

In the Displays panel, add the following displays by right-clicking and selecting Add:

- Map: Set the topic to /map. This will display the output map from your mapping node.
- LaserScan: Set the topic to /scan. This will display the laser scan data being published by your robot or sensor simulation.

You can customize the appearance of these displays using their properties in the Properties panel on the right-hand side.

3. **Load and save your configuration**

To load your new rviz configuration file, go to File -> Open Project and select the .rviz file you created earlier. To save your current configuration, go to File -> Save As.

Now you should be able to visualize mapping outputs in real-time using rviz.

Chapter 14: Path Planning and Navigation

This chapter introduces the ROS Navigation Stack and demonstrates how to write path planning algorithms in Python. We'll also explore how to integrate sensor data for navigation and provide practical examples of autonomous robot navigation.

Introduction to the ROS Navigation Stack

The ROS Navigation Stack is a collection of packages that enable mobile robots to navigate autonomously. It includes modules for localization, mapping, and path planning. To use the navigation stack, you'll need to install it along with your ROS distribution:

```
sudo apt-get update && sudo apt-get install ros-<your_ros_distro>-navigation*
```

After installation, initialize the navigation stack by running:

```
roscore
rosrun map_server map_server <map_file>
roslaunch amcl amcl.launch
roslaunch move_base move_base.launch
```

Replace <map_file> with your robot's map file.

Writing Path Planning Algorithms in Python

Path planning involves finding a collision-free path from the start to the goal position for a robot. ROS provides several packages like move_base and dwa_local_planner for path planning, but you can also write custom algorithms using Python.

Let's create a simple example of a path planner that uses A* algorithm to find a path between two points:

```python
import numpy as np
from nav_msgs.msg import Path
from geometry_msgs.msg import PoseStamped
```

```python
def make_plan(start, goal):
    # Initialize open and closed sets
    open_set = {start}
    closed_set = set()

    # Define cost function (distance to start)
    def f(n):
        return np.linalg.norm(np.array([n.x, n.y]) - np.array([start.x, start.y]))

    while open_set:
        # Find the node with lowest cost in open_set
        current = min(open_set, key=lambda n: f(n) + heuristic(n))

        if current == goal:
            return reconstruct_path(current)

        open_set.remove(current)
        closed_set.add(current)

        for neighbor in get_neighbors(current):
            if neighbor not in closed_set and neighbor not in open_set:
                open_set.add(neighbor)
                neighbor.parent = current

    return []

def heuristic(node):
    # Euclidean distance to goal as heuristic function
    return np.linalg.norm(np.array([node.x, node.y]) - np.array([goal.x, goal.y]))
```

```python
def get_neighbors(node):
    # Get neighboring nodes within robot's sensor range
    pass  # Implement this based on your robot's capabilities


def reconstruct_path(current):
    path = []
    while current is not None:
        path.append(current)
        current = current.parent
    return Path.from_array(path[::-1])


# Example usage:
start = PoseStamped()
goal = PoseStamped()

# Set pose data for start and goal positions
start.header.frame_id = "map"
goal.header.frame_id = "map"

# Publish the planned path
path_publisher = rospy.Publisher('/planned_path', Path, queue_size=1)
rospy.init_node('path_planner')
path = make_plan(start, goal)
path_publisher.publish(path)
```

Integrating Sensor Data for Navigation

To navigate autonomously, robots need to perceive their environment using sensors like lidar, cameras, or encoders. In ROS, sensor data is published as topics that can be subscribed to and processed by your navigation algorithms.

Here's an example of subscribing to a lidar topic and filtering out obstacles:

```python
import rospy
from sensor_msgs.msg import LaserScan


def lidar_callback(msg):
    # Filter out obstacles based on lidar data
    ranges = msg.ranges
    min_range = 0.2  # Minimum range for obstacle detection (meters)
    max_range = 10.0  # Maximum range of lidar sensor (meters)

    obstacles = []
    for i, range in enumerate(ranges):
        if range < min_range or range > max_range:
            continue
        if range < max_range * 0.7:  # Consider values below 70% of max range as obstacles
            obstacles.append((i, range))

    # Process obstacles for navigation (e.g., update path planner)
    pass

# Initialize node and subscribe to lidar topic
rospy.init_node('lidar_processor')
rospy.Subscriber('/scan', LaserScan, lidar_callback)


while not rospy.is_shutdown():
    rospy.spin()
```

Now let's combine the concepts from above to create a practical example of autonomous robot navigation using the move_base package:

1. First, load your robot's map file and initialize the navigation stack as shown in the introduction.
2. Create a Python script (e.g., navigate.py) that contains the following functions:
   - Define a function to send goal positions to the move_base action server.
   - Implement sensor data processing (e.g., lidar filtering) based on your robot's capabilities.
   - Integrate path planning algorithms or use default planners provided by move_base.
3. In your script, initialize ROS nodes and publishers/subscriptions as needed.
4. Define a sequence of goal positions for your robot to navigate through.
5. Implement a main loop that processes sensor data, plans paths, and sends goals to the move_base action server.
6. Run the script on your robot's computer to test autonomous navigation.

Here's an example function to send goals to the move_base action server:

```python
import rospy
from move_base_msgs.msg import MoveBaseActionGoal
from geometry_msgs.msg import PoseStamped


def send_goal(goal_pose):
    goal_msg = MoveBaseActionGoal()
    goal_msg.header.stamp = rospy.Time.now()
    goal_msg.goal.target_pose.pose = goal_pose
    goal_msg.goal.target_pose.header.frame_id = "map"
    goal_publisher.publish(goal_msg)
```

You can adapt this example to suit your robot's capabilities and navigation requirements. Make sure to test your implementation thoroughly before deploying it on a real robot.

That's it for this chapter! In the next chapter, we'll explore advanced topics like multi-robot coordination and swarm intelligence with ROS.

Chapter 15: Advanced Motion Planning with MoveIt!

In this chapter, we will delve into the advanced capabilities of MoveIt!, a popular motion planning framework for robotics, when used in conjunction with Python. We'll start by setting up MoveIt! with our robotic arm and then move on to writing Python scripts for controlling its motion. Finally, we'll explore practical examples of complex motion planning tasks.

Setting Up MoveIt!

Before we begin, ensure you have ROS installed and properly configured. If not, follow the official ROS installation guide (https://wiki.ros.org/ROS/Installation) to set it up on your system.

To install MoveIt!, use the following commands in your terminal:

```
sudo apt-get update && sudo apt-get install ros-<ros_distro>-moveit
```

Replace <ros_distro> with your ROS distribution (e.g., noetic, melodic, etc.).

After installation, you can initialize a new workspace and build it:

```
mkdir -p ~/catkin_ws/src
cd ~/catkin_ws/src
git clone https://github.com/ros-planning/moveit_resources.git
cd ..
catkin_make
```

Now we're ready to use MoveIt! with Python.

Writing Python Scripts for Robotic Arm Control

First, let's import the necessary modules and initialize a MoveGroupCommander object to control our robotic arm:

```
import moveit_commander
import geometry_msgs.msg
```

```python
# Initialize MoveIt Commander
moveit_commander.roscpp_init()
robot = moveit_commander.RobotCommander()

# Get the arm group
group_name = "manipulator"
move_group = moveit_commander.MoveGroupCommander(group_name)
```

Here, we've initialized the MoveIt Commander and obtained a reference to our robotic arm's MoveGroupCommander object.

Let's define a function to plan and execute a motion:

```python
def plan_and_execute(target_pose):
    # Plan to target pose
    move_group.set_pose_target(target_pose)
    plan = move_group.plan()

    # Execute the plan
    move_group.go(wait=True)

    # Clear the target pose
    move_group.clear_pose_targets()
```

This function takes a geometry_msgs.msg.PoseStamped object as input, plans to that target pose using the move_group.set_pose_target() method, and then executes the planned motion.

Practical Examples of Complex Motion Planning

Now let's explore some practical examples of complex motion planning tasks.

Example 1: Pick-and-Place Motion

In this example, we'll demonstrate a pick-and-place motion where the robotic arm picks up an object from one location and places it in another:

```python
# Define target poses
pick_pose = geometry_msgs.msg.PoseStamped()
pick_pose.header.frame_id = "base_link"
pick_pose.pose.position.x = 0.2
pick_pose.pose.position.y = 0.0
pick_pose.pose.position.z = 0.1


place_pose = geometry_msgs.msg.PoseStamped()
place_pose.header.frame_id = "base_link"
place_pose.pose.position.x = 0.4
place_pose.pose.position.y = 0.2
place_pose.pose.position.z = 0.2


# Plan and execute pick motion
plan_and_execute(pick_pose)


# Plan and execute place motion
plan_and_execute(place_pose)
```

Example 2: Obstacle Avoidance Motion

In this example, we'll demonstrate how MoveIt! can plan motions to avoid obstacles:

```python
# Define target pose with obstacle in the way
target_pose = geometry_msgs.msg.PoseStamped()
target_pose.header.frame_id = "base_link"
target_pose.pose.position.x = 0.3
target_pose.pose.position.y = -0.1
target_pose.pose.position.z = 0.2
```

```python
# Plan to target pose with obstacle avoidance
move_group.set_pose_target(target_pose)
plan = move_group.plan(avoid_collisions=True)

# Execute the plan
move_group.go(wait=True)

# Clear the target pose
move_group.clear_pose_targets()
```

In this example, we've added an obstacle by setting avoid_collisions to True in the plan() method call. MoveIt! will then generate a collision-free motion plan.

Example 3: Cartesian Impedance Control Motion

In this example, we'll demonstrate how to use Cartesian impedance control for smooth, compliant motion:

```python
# Define target pose
target_pose = geometry_msgs.msg.PoseStamped()
target_pose.header.frame_id = "base_link"
target_pose.pose.position.x = 0.3
target_pose.pose.position.y = 0.1
target_pose.pose.position.z = 0.2

# Plan to target pose with Cartesian impedance control
move_group.set_pose_target(target_pose)
plan = move_group.plan()
plan[0].cartesianImpedance.stiffness = [0.5, 0.5, 0.5]
plan[0].cartesianImpedance.damping = [0.1, 0.1, 0.1]

# Execute the plan
```

```python
move_group.go(wait=True)

# Clear the target pose
move_group.clear_pose_targets()
```

In this example, we've set Cartesian stiffness and damping values for impedance control during motion planning.

And that's it! You now have a solid foundation in advanced motion planning with MoveIt! using Python.

Chapter 16: Real-Time Systems in Python

ROS (Robot Operating System) is designed to handle real-time systems, and Python is often used for scripting and high-level control. However, implementing real-time systems with Python in ROS can be challenging due to the global interpreter lock (GIL), which allows only one thread to execute at a time. In this chapter, we will discuss how to implement real-time systems using Python in ROS, focusing on ros_control for real-time loops and practical examples of real-time robotic control.

Implementing Real-Time Systems with Python in ROS

To overcome the GIL limitation in Python, we can use multithreading or multiprocessing. However, these methods can introduce complex issues like race conditions and deadlocks. A simpler approach is to use ROS's built-in facilities for handling real-time systems.

ROS provides several nodes that can run at a specific rate, ensuring deterministic execution times. Here's an example of creating a simple publisher node that publishes a message at a specified rate:

```python
import rospy
from std_msgs.msg import String

def talker():
    pub = rospy.Publisher('chatter', String, queue_size=10)
    rospy.init_node('talker', anonymous=True)
    rate = rospy.Rate(10)  # Set the publish rate to 10 Hz
    while not rospy.is_shutdown():
        hello_str = "hello world %s" % rospy.get_time()
        rospy.loginfo(hello_str)
        pub.publish(hello_str)
        rate.sleep()
```

```python
if __name__ == '__main__':
    try:
        talker()
    except rospy.ROSInterruptException:
        pass
```

In this example, the rospy.Rate object ensures that the message is published at a frequency of 10 Hz (once every 0.1 seconds). The rate.sleep() call enforces the desired publishing rate.

Using ros_control for Real-Time Loops

The ros_control package provides a way to implement real-time control loops in ROS using Python. It allows you to create controllers that run at specified rates, ensuring deterministic execution times. Here's an example of creating a simple position controller for a robotic arm using ros_control:

1. First, create a transmission_interface/SimpleTransmission file (e.g., simple_transmission.yaml) with the following content:

```yaml
type: SimpleTransmission
hardware_interface: EffortJoyvelHWInterface
joints:
 - joint_name: arm_joint_1
   velocity_limits:
     max_velocity: 2.0
```

2. Create a ros_control controller configuration file (e.g., arm_controller.yaml) with the following content:

```yaml
controller_manager_ns: ''
controller_list:
 - name: 'arm_position_controller'
   action: FollowJointTrajectory
   type: position_controllers/JointPositionController
```

```yaml
joints:
  - arm_joint_1
```

3. Create a Python script (arm_control.py) that uses the ros_control interface to send commands to the robotic arm:

```python
import rospy
from trajectory_msgs.msg import JointTrajectory, JointTrajectoryPoint


def move_arm():
    pub = rospy.Publisher('/arm_controller/command', JointTrajectory, queue_size=1)
    rospy.init_node('arm_control', anonymous=True)
    rate = rospy.Rate(50)  # Set the control rate to 50 Hz
    while not rospy.is_shutdown():
        msg = JointTrajectory()
        msg.header.stamp = rospy.Time.now()
        msg.joint_names = ['arm_joint_1']

        point = JointTrajectoryPoint()
        point.positions = [rospy.get_time()]  # Set the desired position to the current time
        point.velocities = []
        point.accelerations = []
        msg.points.append(point)

        pub.publish(msg)
        rate.sleep()


if __name__ == '__main__':
    try:
        move_arm()
    except rospy.ROSInterruptException:
        pass
```

In this example, the JointTrajectory message is published at a frequency of 50 Hz (rospy.Rate(50)). The desired position for arm_joint_1 is set to the current time (rospy.get_time()), which will cause the arm to move continuously.

Practical Example: Real-Time Robotic Control

Now let's combine our knowledge to create a practical example of real-time robotic control. In this example, we'll use a simple differential drive robot (like TurtleBot) and implement a PID controller to follow a wall using Python in ROS.

1. First, make sure you have the turtlebot_rviz_launchers package installed:

```
sudo apt-get install ros-<your_ros_distro>-turtlebot-rviz-launchers
```

2. Create a new launch file (wall_follower.launch) with the following content:

```xml
<?xml version="1.0"?>
<launch>
  <arg name="scan_topic" default="/scan"/>
  <arg name="cmd_vel_topic" default="/mobile_base/commands/velocity"/>

  <!-- Publish wall distance sensor data -->
  <node pkg="turtlebot_wall_follower" type="wall_distance_sensor.py" name="wall_distance_sensor">
    <param name="scan_topic" value="${arg_scan_topic}"/>
    <param name="min_range" value="0.3"/>
    <param name="max_range" value="1.5"/>
  </node>

  <!-- PID controller for wall following -->
  <node pkg="turtlebot_wall_follower" type="wall_pid_controller.py" name="wall_pid_controller">
    <rosparam command="load" file="$(find turtlebot_wall_follower)/config/pid.yaml"/>
    <param name="scan_topic" value="${arg_scan_topic}"/>
    <param name="cmd_vel_topic" value="${arg_cmd_vel_topic}"/>
```

```
</node>

<!-- Launch RVIZ -->
<include file="$(find turtlebot_rviz_launchers)/view_navi.rviz"/>
</launch>
```

3. Create a Python script (wall_distance_sensor.py) that publishes the distance to the nearest wall:

```python
import rospy
from sensor_msgs.msg import LaserScan
from geometry_msgs.msg import PoseStamped


def main():
    rospy.init_node('wall_distance_sensor')
    pub = rospy.Publisher('/wall_distance', PoseStamped, queue_size=1)

    scan_topic = rospy.get_param('~scan_topic')
    min_range = rospy.get_param('~min_range')
    max_range = rospy.get_param('~max_range')

    rate = rospy.Rate(10)  # Set the publish rate to 10 Hz
    while not rospy.is_shutdown():
        msg = PoseStamped()
        msg.header.stamp = rospy.Time.now()

        scan_msg = rospy.wait_for_message(scan_topic, LaserScan)
        front_distance = min(scan_msg.ranges[0:360])  # Get the minimum distance from
the front

        if front_distance > min_range and front_distance < max_range:
            msg.pose.position.x = front_distance
            pub.publish(msg)
```

```
        rate.sleep()


if __name__ == '__main__':
    try:
        main()
    except rospy.ROSInterruptException:
        pass
```

4. Create a Python script (wall_pid_controller.py) that implements the PID controller for wall following:

```
import rospy
from geometry_msgs.msg import PoseStamped, Twist


class WallFollower:
    def __init__(self):
        self.desired_distance = 1.0
        self.kp = rospy.get_param('~kp')
        self.ki = rospy.get_param('~ki')
        self.kd = rospy.get_param('~kd')

        self.error_sum = 0.0
        self.prev_error = 0.0
        self.integral = 0.0

        scan_topic = rospy.get_param('~scan_topic')
        cmd_vel_topic = rospy.get_param('~cmd_vel_topic')

        self.distance_sub = rospy.Subscriber(scan_topic, PoseStamped,
self.distance_callback)
        self.cmd_vel_pub = rospy.Publisher(cmd_vel_topic, Twist, queue_size=1)
```

```python
def distance_callback(self, msg):
    error = self.desired_distance - msg.pose.position.x
    self.error_sum += error

    derivative = error - self.prev_error
    self.prev_error = error

    self.integral = self.ki * self.error_sum
    pid_output = self.kp * error + self.integral + self.kd * derivative

    twist_msg = Twist()
    twist_msg.linear.x = pid_output
    twist_msg.angular.z = -pid_output / 10.0
    self.cmd_vel_pub.publish(twist_msg)

def run(self):
    rate = rospy.Rate(50)  # Set the control rate to 50 Hz
    while not rospy.is_shutdown():
        rate.sleep()

if __name__ == '__main__':
    rospy.init_node('wall_pid_controller')
    follower = WallFollower()
    follower.run()
```

5. Create a PID configuration file (pid.yaml) in the turtlebot_wall_follower/config folder with the following content:

```yaml
kp: 0.5
ki: 0.1
kd: 0.2
```

6. Launch the wall follower system using the launch file created earlier:

```
roslaunch turtlebot_wall_follower wall_follower.launch
```

7. Open RVIZ and select the view_navi.rviz configuration file located in the turtlebot_rviz_launchers package to visualize the wall following process.

This practical example demonstrates real-time robotic control using Python in ROS with the help of ros_control. The PID controller runs at a frequency of 50 Hz, ensuring deterministic execution times and allowing the robot to follow the wall smoothly.

Chapter 17: Multi-Robot Systems

This chapter introduces you to the world of multi-robot systems using ROS (Robot Operating System) and Python. We'll cover writing Python nodes for multi-robot coordination, managing multiple robots with tf2, and explore practical examples of cooperative multi-robot systems.

Writing Python Nodes for Multi-Robot Coordination

In multi-robot systems, each robot typically has its own ROS node running on it. To coordinate these robots, we need to write Python nodes that can communicate with other nodes on different machines or within the same network.

Publisher/Subscriber Model

ROS uses a publisher/subscriber model for inter-process communication. Each robot can publish data topics, and other robots can subscribe to those topics to receive the data.

Here's an example of publishing and subscribing to a topic using Python:

```python
import rospy
from geometry_msgs.msg import PoseStamped


def talker():
    pub = rospy.Publisher('robot1_pose', PoseStamped, queue_size=10)
    rospy.init_node('talker', anonymous=True)
    rate = rospy.Rate(10) # 10hz
    while not rospy.is_shutdown():
        pose_msg = PoseStamped()
        # fill the pose message...
        pub.publish(pose_msg)
        rate.sleep()
```

```python
def listener():
    rospy.init_node('listener', anonymous=True)
    rospy.Subscriber('robot1_pose', PoseStamped, callback)
    rospy.spin()

def callback(data):
    rospy.loginfo("Robot 1 Pose: %s", data)

if __name__ == '__main__':
    try:
        talker()
    except rospy.ROSInterruptException:
        pass

    try:
        listener()
    except rospy.ROSInterruptException:
        pass
```

In this example, talker publishes the pose of robot 1 on topic 'robot1_pose', and listener subscribes to that topic to receive the pose data.

Service Model

Sometimes, we need more complex interaction between robots where a request/response model is required. ROS provides services for this purpose.

Here's an example of a service server and client using Python:

```python
import rospy
from multi_robot_srvs.srv import RequestPose, RequestPoseResponse

def handle_request_pose(req):
    # perform some action based on req
```

```python
    pose_response = PoseStamped()
    # fill the pose message...
    return RequestPoseResponse(pose_response)

def server():
    rospy.init_node('server')
    s = rospy.Service('request_pose', RequestPose, handle_request_pose)
    rospy.spin()

def client():
    rospy.wait_for_service('request_pose')
    try:
        request_pose = rospy.ServiceProxy('request_pose', RequestPose)
        resp1 = request_pose(0) # request pose for robot 0
        rospy.loginfo("Robot Pose: %s", resp1.pose)
    except rospy.ServiceException, e:
        print "Service call failed: %s" % e

if __name__ == "__main__":
    server()
    client()
```

In this example, the service server handles requests for robot poses and returns them to the client.

Using tf2 for Managing Multiple Robots

tf2 (or transform tree 2) is used to manage transformations between robots in a multi-robot system. It allows us to query the pose of one robot with respect to another.

Here's an example of using tf2 to get the pose of robot 1 relative to robot 0:

```python
import rospy
from geometry_msgs.msg import TransformStamped
```

```python
from tf2_ros import TransformListener, Buffer

def callback(data):
    # perform some action based on data.transform
    pass


if __name__ == "__main__":
    rospy.init_node('tf2_listener')
    buffer = Buffer()
    listener = TransformListener(buffer)
    rate = rospy.Rate(10)

    while not rospy.is_shutdown():
        try:
            trans = buffer.lookupTransform('/robot0', '/robot1', rospy.Time(0))
            pose_msg = TransformStamped()
            pose_msg.transform.translation.x = trans[0]
            pose_msg.transform.translation.y = trans[1]
            pose_msg.transform.translation.z = trans[2]
            pose_msg.transform.rotation = trans[3] # assuming quaternion is returned as a
tuple
            callback(pose_msg)
        except (tf2_ros.LookupError, tf2_ros.ConnectivityException) as e:
            print(e)

        rate.sleep()
```

In this example, the lookupTransform function is used to get the pose of robot 1 relative to robot 0.

Let's explore a practical example of cooperative multi-robot systems: *Formation Control*.

Formation Control Example

In formation control, each robot maintains a certain distance and orientation with respect to other robots in the formation. We'll demonstrate this using two robots, robot 0 (leader) and robot 1 (follower).

First, let's define a service for sending commands to robot 1:

```python
import rospy
from multi_robot_srvs.srv import MoveToPose, MoveToPoseRequest


def move_to_pose_client(pose):
    rospy.wait_for_service('move_to_pose')
    try:
        move_to_pose = rospy.ServiceProxy('move_to_pose', MoveToPose)
        resp1 = move_to_pose(MoveToPoseRequest(pose))
        return resp1.success
    except rospy.ServiceException, e:
        print "Service call failed: %s" % e
        return False


if __name__ == "__main__":
    pose = PoseStamped()
    # fill the pose message...
    move_to_pose_client(pose)
```

Now, let's implement formation control:

```python
import rospy
from geometry_msgs.msg import PoseStamped
from tf2_ros import TransformListener, Buffer
```

```python
def follower():
    buffer = Buffer()
    listener = TransformListener(buffer)


    # initialize robot 1 pose to current pose
    robot1_pose = PoseStamped()


    rate = rospy.Rate(10)
    while not rospy.is_shutdown():
        try:
            trans = buffer.lookupTransform('/robot0', '/robot1', rospy.Time(0))
            desired_pose = PoseStamped()
            desired_pose.pose.position.x = trans[0] + 2 # maintain a distance of 2 meters
            desired_pose.pose.position.y = trans[1]
            desired_pose.pose.orientation = robot1_pose.pose.orientation # maintain
orientation
            if move_to_pose_client(desired_pose):
                robot1_pose = desired_pose
        except (tf2_ros.LookupError, tf2_ros.ConnectivityException) as e:
            print(e)


        rate.sleep()


if __name__ == "__main__":
    rospy.init_node('follower')
    follower()
```

In this example, robot 1 follows robot 0 while maintaining a distance of 2 meters.

This is just one example of cooperative multi-robot systems. There are many other applications such as swarm robotics, multi-robot mapping, and search-and-rescue operations that can be implemented using ROS and Python.

That's all for this chapter! In the next chapter, we'll explore working with sensors in ROS using Python.

Chapter 18: Machine Learning Integration

ROS (Robot Operating System) is a robust framework for building robot applications. Its flexibility extends to integrating with machine learning frameworks like TensorFlow and PyTorch, enabling robots to learn from their environment and improve performance over time.

To integrate Python-based machine learning frameworks with ROS, you'll need to create a ROS node that publishes sensor data, subscribes to topics containing relevant information, and uses an ML model to make decisions or predictions. Here's a step-by-step guide using TensorFlow as an example:

1. **Setup your workspace**: Create a ROS workspace if you haven't already, and source the setup file: source /opt/ros/noetic/setup.bash (replace 'noetic' with your ROS distribution).

2. **Install necessary packages**:

   pip install tensorflow
   rosdep install --from-paths src --ignore-src --rosdistro noetic -y

3. **Create a new Python node**: Create a new Python file in your package's src folder, e.g., ml_node.py.

4. **Import necessary libraries**:

   ```
   import rospy
   from sensor_msgs.msg import Image
   import tensorflow as tf
   ```

5. **Load your TensorFlow model**:

   ```
   # Assume you have a saved TensorFlow model in 'path/to/model'
   model = tf.keras.models.load_model('path/to/model')
   ```

6. **Create ROS publishers and subscribers**:

```
pub = rospy.Publisher('/predictions', Image, queue_size=10)
sub = rospy.Subscriber('/camera/image_raw', Image, callback_function)
```

7. **Define the callback function**: This function will be called whenever new data arrives on the subscribed topic.

```
def callback_function(data):
    # Preprocess data as needed for your model (e.g., resizing, normalization)
    processed_data = preprocess_data(data)

    # Make predictions using the TensorFlow model
    prediction = model.predict(processed_data)

    # Publish the prediction on the ROS topic
    pub.publish(prediction)
```

8. **Initialize and spin the node**:

```
def main():
    rospy.init_node('ml_node', anonymous=True)
    rospy.spin()


if __name__ == '__main__':
    try:
        main()
    except rospy.ROSInterruptException:
        pass
```

Writing Python Nodes to Deploy ML Models

To write a Python node that deploys an ML model, follow these steps:

1. **Import necessary libraries**:

```python
import rospy
from std_msgs.msg import Float64MultiArray
import numpy as np
import your_ml_library  # Import the library containing your trained ML model
```

2. **Load your ML model**:

```python
ml_model = your_ml_library.load('path/to/your/model.pkl')  # Assuming your
model is saved as a pickle file
```

3. **Create ROS publishers and subscribers**:

```python
pub = rospy.Publisher('/predictions', Float64MultiArray, queue_size=10)
sub = rospy.Subscriber('/sensor_data', Float64MultiArray, callback_function)
```

4. **Define the callback function**:

```python
def callback_function(data):
    # Convert ROS message to NumPy array
    np_array = np.array(data.data)

    # Make predictions using your ML model
    prediction = ml_model.predict(np_array)

    # Publish the prediction on the ROS topic as a Float64MultiArray message
    msg = Float64MultiArray()
    msg.data = prediction.tolist()
    pub.publish(msg)
```

5. **Initialize and spin the node**:

```python
def main():
    rospy.init_node('ml_deployment_node', anonymous=True)
    rospy.spin()
```

```
if __name__ == '__main__':
    try:
        main()
    except rospy.ROSInterruptException:
        pass
```

Practical Examples of AI-Enhanced Robotic Behavior

Let's explore two practical examples of AI-enhanced robotic behavior using ROS and machine learning.

Example 1: Object Recognition

In this example, we'll use a pre-trained YOLO model for real-time object recognition with a robot camera feed. We'll publish the bounding boxes of detected objects on a ROS topic.

1. **Install OpenCV**: You'll need OpenCV to work with images and process YOLO outputs.

   ```
   pip install opencv-python
   ```

2. **Modify ml_node.py** to include YOLO object detection:

   ```python
   import rospy
   from sensor_msgs.msg import Image
   import cv2
   import numpy as np

   # Load YOLO pre-trained weights and config file
   net = cv2.dnn.readNet("path/to/yolov3.weights", "path/to/yolov3.cfg")

   def callback_function(data):
       # Process image data to prepare it for YOLO
       frame = np.frombuffer(data.data, dtype=np.uint8).reshape(data.height,
   ```

```
    data.width, -1)

        # Perform object detection using YOLO
    blob = cv2.dnn.blobFromImage(frame, 1/255, (416, 416), (0, 0, 0), True,
crop=False)
    net.setInput(blob)
    outs = net.forward(net.getUnconnectedOutLayersNames())

        # Process YOLO outputs and publish bounding boxes on ROS topic
    pub.publish(process_yolo_outputs(outs[0], frame.shape))

def process_yolo_outputs(outputs, image_shape):
    # ... (process_yolo_outputs function implementation)
    pass

# ... (rest of the node initialization remains the same)
```

3. **Launch the ROS node**:

```
rosrun your_package_name ml_node.py
```

In this example, we'll use a trained LSTM model to predict robot motion based on past velocity data. We'll publish predicted velocities on a ROS topic for real-time robot control.

1. **Modify ml_node.py** to include LSTM-based predictive motion planning:

```
import rospy
from geometry_msgs.msg import Vector3
import numpy as np
import your_ml_library  # Import the library containing your trained LSTM model
```

```python
ml_model = your_ml_library.load('path/to/your/lstm_model.pkl')

velocity_history = []  # Store past velocities for prediction

def callback_function(data):
    global velocity_history
    current_velocity = np.array([data.x, data.y, data.z])  # Extract x, y, z velocities
from ROS message
    velocity_history.append(current_velocity)

    if len(velocity_history) > 100:  # Predict only after collecting enough historical
data
        predicted_velocities = ml_model.predict(np.array(velocity_history[-100:]))[-1]

        # Publish predicted velocities on ROS topic as Vector3 message
        msg = Vector3()
        msg.x, msg.y, msg.z = predicted_velocities.tolist()
        pub.publish(msg)

# ... (rest of the node initialization remains the same)
```

2. **Launch the ROS node:**

```
rosrun your_package_name ml_node.py
```

Chapter 19: Advanced Simulation and Testing

In this chapter, we will explore advanced topics in ROS simulation using Python. We will discuss how to write Python plugins for Gazebo simulations, automate simulation workflows with Python scripts, test Python nodes using unittest and rostest, and provide practical examples of simulation-driven development.

Writing Python Plugins for Gazebo Simulations

Gazebo is a powerful 3D robotics simulator that can be extended via plugins. These plugins can be written in C++, but it's also possible to use Python with the help of the python-binding package. Here's an example of a simple Python plugin that prints messages every second:

```python
from gazebo.plugins import *

class MyPlugin(Plugin):
    def __init__(self, name, node):
        super().__init__(name, node)
        self.update_period = 1.0

    def update(self):
        print("Hello from Gazebo Python plugin!")

def load(so_name, model_path, scene_num):
    return MyPlugin(so_name, model_path, scene_num)

GazeboRegisterPlugin(MyPlugin)
```

To use this plugin:

1. Save the code in a file named my_plugin.py.
2. Build the plugin with python setup.py install.

3. Load it in Gazebo using the following command: gazebo --plugin-path plugins --model-path models -s plugins/my_plugin.py.

Automating Simulation Workflows with Python Scripts

Automating simulation workflows can save time and increase efficiency. Here's an example of a Python script that starts a Gazebo simulation, waits for some time, publishes messages to a topic, and then stops the simulation:

```python
import rospy
from gazebo_msgs.srv import Empty


def run_simulation():
    # Initialize ROS node
    rospy.init_node('simulation_control')

    # StartGazebo service call
    start_gazebo = rospy.ServiceProxy('/gazebo/start', Empty)
    start_gazebo()

    print("Simulation started")

    # Wait for 5 seconds
    rospy.sleep(5.0)

    # Publish messages to a topic
    pub = rospy.Publisher('my_topic', String, queue_size=10)
    rate = rospy.Rate(1)  # 1 Hz
    while not rospy.is_shutdown():
        msg = "Hello from Python script!"
        pub.publish(msg)
        rate.sleep()
```

```python
    print("Published messages")

    # StopGazebo service call
    stop_gazebo = rospy.ServiceProxy('/gazebo/stop', Empty)
    stop_gazebo()

    print("Simulation stopped")

if __name__ == '__main__':
    try:
        run_simulation()
    except rospy.ROSInterruptException:
        pass
```

Unit testing is crucial for ensuring the correctness of your code. ROS provides unittest for unit tests and rostest for integration tests.

Here's an example of a simple Python node that adds two integers:

```python
import rospy
from my_pkg.msg import Int64

def add_two_ints(data):
    result = data.data1 + data.data2
    pub.publish(result)

if __name__ == '__main__':
    rospy.init_node('add_two_int_node')
    pub = rospy.Publisher('result', Int64, queue_size=10)
```

```
rospy.Subscriber('input', Int64, add_two_ints)
rospy.spin()
```

And here's a corresponding unit test using unittest:

```python
import unittest
from my_pkg.msg import Int64

class TestAddTwoInts(unittest.TestCase):
    def test_addition(self):
        data = Int64(data1=2, data2=3)
        result = add_two_ints(data)
        self.assertEqual(result.data, 5)


if __name__ == '__main__':
    unittest.main()
```

To run the unit tests, save them in a file named test_add_two_int.py and use the following command:

```
rosrun my_pkg test_add_two_int.py
```

For integration testing with rostest, create a test suite XML file (my_test_suite.xml) containing the following content:

```xml
<rosunit>
  <test name="add_two_int_node_test" type="rospy rostest add_two_int_test" />
</rosunit>
```

Then, run the tests using the following command:

```
rosrun my_pkg my_test_suite.xml
```

Simulation-driven development involves designing and testing systems in simulation before deploying them on real hardware. Here's a practical example using ROS and Gazebo:

1. **Create a robot model**: First, create a simple robot model with two wheels using the Gazebo robot model editor.

2. **Export the model**: Export the model as an SDF file (e.g., my_robot.sdf).

3. **Write a Python node for driving the robot**: Create a ROS node that publishes velocity commands to the /cmd_vel topic based on user input:

```python
import rospy
from geometry_msgs.msg import Twist


def drive_robot():
    pub = rospy.Publisher('cmd_vel', Twist, queue_size=10)
    rospy.init_node('drive_robot')
    rate = rospy.Rate(1)  # 1 Hz

    while not rospy.is_shutdown():
        twist = Twist()
        twist.linear.x = input("Enter linear velocity (m/s): ")
        twist.angular.z = input("Enter angular velocity (rad/s): ")
        pub.publish(twist)
        rate.sleep()


if __name__ == '__main__':
    try:
        drive_robot()
```

```
except rospy.ROSInterruptException:
    pass
```

4. **Simulate the robot**: Launch Gazebo with your robot model and run the drive_robot.py node using the following commands:

```
roscore
gazebo my_robot.sdf
rosrun my_pkg drive_robot.py
```

5. **Test the robot in simulation**: Use the keyboard or a joystick to control the robot's movement, and observe its behavior in Gazebo.

6. **Deploy on real hardware (optional)**: Once you're satisfied with the performance in simulation, deploy the same ROS node on your real robot hardware for further testing and validation.

By following these practices, you can develop more reliable robotics systems by leveraging the power of ROS and Gazebo simulations.

Chapter 20: Distributed Systems with ROS

In this chapter, we will explore how to create distributed robotic systems using the Robot Operating System (ROS) and Python. We'll start by writing Python nodes that can communicate with each other over a network, then delve into synchronizing nodes across multiple robots, and finally, present practical examples of distributed robotic systems.

Writing Python Nodes for Distributed Systems

To create distributed systems with ROS, we first need to understand how to write Python nodes that can communicate with each other. In ROS, nodes are the basic building blocks of a system, and they communicate using topics (for publishing/subscription) or services (for request/response).

Here's a simple example of two Python nodes communicating over a topic:

Node 1: Publisher

```python
import rospy
from std_msgs.msg import String

def talker():
    pub = rospy.Publisher('chatter', String, queue_size=10)
    rospy.init_node('talker', anonymous=True)
    rate = rospy.Rate(10) # 10 Hz

    while not rospy.is_shutdown():
        hello_str = "hello world %s" % rospy.get_time()
        pub.publish(hello_str)
        rate.sleep()

if __name__ == '__main__':
    try:
```

```
    talker()
except rospy.ROSInterruptException:
    pass
```

Node 2: Subscriber

```python
import rospy
from std_msgs.msg import String

def callback(data):
    rospy.loginfo("Received message: %s", data.data)

def listener():
    rospy.init_node('listener', anonymous=True)
    rospy.Subscriber('chatter', String, callback)

    # spin() keeps the node from exiting until it's explicitly shutdown
    rospy.spin()

if __name__ == '__main__':
    listener()
```

To run these nodes on separate machines:

1. Set up ROS master and network communication following the ROS installation guide.

2. Run talker.py on one machine.

3. Run listener.py on another machine, connected to the same ROS network.

Synchronizing Nodes Across Multiple Robots

Synchronizing nodes across multiple robots involves coordinating actions among different robotic platforms. ROS provides several ways to achieve this, such as action servers/clients, synchronization primitives (lock, barrier), and distributed multi-robot systems using Multi-Master-Fallback.

Here's an example of synchronizing two robots using actionlib:

Robot 1: Action Server

```python
import rospy
import actionlib
from geometry_msgs.msg import TwistAction, TwistGoal


def move_forward(goal):
    twist = Twist()
    twist.linear.x = 0.2
    rate = rospy.Rate(10)
    while not goal.is_active():
        pub.publish(twist)
        rate.sleep()
    rate.sleep()


if __name__ == '__main__':
    rospy.init_node('robot_1_action_server')
    server = actionlib.SimpleActionServer('move_forward', TwistAction,
execute_done_cb=move_forward, auto_start=False)
    server.start()
    rospy.spin()
```

Robot 2: Action Client

```python
import rospy
import actionlib
from geometry_msgs.msg import TwistAction, TwistGoal


def goal_callback(goal):
```

```python
    print "Received goal with target position:", goal.target_position

if __name__ == '__main__':
    rospy.init_node('robot_2_action_client')
    client = actionlib.SimpleActionClient('move_forward', TwistAction)
    client.wait_for_server()

    goal = TwistGoal()
    goal.target_position = 1.0
    client.send_goal(goal, feedback_cb=goal_callback)
    rospy.spin()
```

To run these nodes:

1. Run robot_1_action_server.py on Robot 1.
2. Run robot_2_action_client.py on Robot 2.

Now let's explore a practical example of a distributed robotic system: **Swarm Navigation**.

Node 1: Leader

The leader node publishes desired waypoints using a ROS topic (waypoints).

```python
import rospy
from geometry_msgs.msg import PointStamped

def publish_waypoints():
    pub = rospy.Publisher('waypoints', PointStamped, queue_size=10)
    rospy.init_node('leader')
    rate = rospy.Rate(5)  # 5 Hz

    while not rospy.is_shutdown():
```

```python
        waypoint = PointStamped()
        waypoint.point.x = ...  # Set desired x coordinate
        waypoint.point.y = ...  # Set desired y coordinate
        pub.publish(waypoint)
        rate.sleep()


if __name__ == '__main__':
    publish_waypoints()
```

Node 2-n: Followers

Each follower node subscribes to the leader's waypoints topic and moves towards them using the move_base package.

```python
import rospy
from geometry_msgs.msg import PointStamped
from move_base_msgs.msg import MoveBaseAction, MoveBaseGoal


def follow_waypoints(waypoint):
    goal = MoveBaseGoal()
    goal.target_pose.header.frame_id = "map"
    goal.target_pose.pose.position.x = waypoint.point.x
    goal.target_pose.pose.position.y = waypoint.point.y
    move_base_client.send_goal(goal)
    rospy.loginfo("Moving towards waypoint")
    move_base_client.wait_for_result()


if __name__ == '__main__':
    rospy.init_node('follower')
    rospy.Subscriber('waypoints', PointStamped, follow_waypoints)

    move_base_client = actionlib.SimpleActionClient('move_base', MoveBaseAction)
```

```
move_base_client.wait_for_server()
rospy.spin()
```

To run this swarm navigation example:

1. Run leader.py on the leader robot.
2. Run follower.py on each follower robot.

This chapter covered creating distributed systems with ROS using Python, including writing nodes for communication, synchronizing robots, and exploring a practical swarm navigation example. In your own projects, consider these principles to create more complex distributed robotic systems.

Chapter 21: ROS for IoT and Cloud Integration

In this chapter, we will explore how to integrate Robot Operating System (ROS) with Internet of Things (IoT) platforms and cloud services. We will focus on Python as the primary language for interfacing these systems. This chapter is divided into three main sections:

1. **Using ROS with IoT Platforms**
2. **Integrating ROS with Cloud Services**
3. **Practical Examples: Remote Monitoring and Control**

1. Using ROS with IoT Platforms

To interface ROS with an IoT platform, we'll use the MQTT (Message Queuing Telemetry Transport) protocol. MQTT is lightweight, easy to implement, and perfect for real-time data transfer in resource-constrained environments.

MQTT Broker Setup

First, set up an MQTT broker like Mosquitto on your ROS system. Here's how you can install it on Ubuntu:

```
sudo apt-get update && sudo apt-get install -y mosquitto mosquitto-clients
```

Python MQTT Client Library

We'll use the paho-mqtt Python library to publish/subscribe to topics.

```
pip install paho-mqtt
```

ROS-IoT Interface Example

Let's create a simple example where a ROS node publishes data to an MQTT topic, and another node subscribes to that topic.

Publisher Node (mqtt_publisher.py):

```python
import rospy
from std_msgs.msg import String
import paho.mqtt.client as mqtt


def on_connect(client, userdata, flags, rc):
    print("Connected with result code "+str(rc))
    client.subscribe("ros_iot_topic")


def on_message(client, userdata, msg):
    print(msg.payload)


def mqtt_publish():
    rospy.init_node('mqtt_publisher', anonymous=True)
    pub = rospy.Publisher('/ros_mqtt_topic', String, queue_size=10)
    rate = rospy.Rate(1) # 1 Hz

    client = mqtt.Client()
    client.on_connect = on_connect
    client.connect("localhost", 1883, 60)

    while not rospy.is_shutdown():
        hello_str = "hello world %s" % rospy.get_time()
        pub.publish(hello_str)
        client.publish("ros_iot_topic", hello_str)
        rate.sleep()


if __name__ == '__main__':
    try:
        mqtt_publish()
    except rospy.ROSInterruptException:
        pass
```

Subscriber Node (mqtt_subscriber.py):

```python
import rospy
from std_msgs.msg import String
import paho.mqtt.client as mqtt


def on_connect(client, userdata, flags, rc):
    print("Connected with result code "+str(rc))
    client.subscribe("/ros_mqtt_topic")


def on_message(client, userdata, msg):
    print(msg.payload)


def callback(data):
    rospy.loginfo(rospy.get_caller_id() + "I heard %s", data.data)


def mqtt_subscribe():
    rospy.init_node('mqtt_subscriber', anonymous=True)
    rospy.Subscriber("/ros_mqtt_topic", String, callback)

    client = mqtt.Client()
    client.on_connect = on_connect
    client.connect("localhost", 1883, 60)

    while not rospy.is_shutdown():
        client.loop()


if __name__ == '__main__':
    try:
        mqtt_subscribe()
    except rospy.ROSInterruptException:
        pass
```

Next, we'll integrate ROS with cloud services like AWS and Azure. For this chapter, we'll focus on Amazon Web Services (AWS) using the RoboMQ service.

RoboMQ Setup

First, sign up for an account on RoboMQ. After creating a free instance, note down your Instance ID and API Key.

Install ROS Bridge

ROS Bridge is a ROS-independent MQTT bridge that allows ROS nodes to communicate using MQTT. Install it using:

```
pip install rosbridge-suite
rosrun rosbridge_server rosbridge_websocket.py --port 9090
```

Connect RoboMQ to ROS Bridge

Follow the steps in the RoboMQ Documentation to connect your RoboMQ instance to the ROS Bridge.

Now, let's create a practical example of remote monitoring and control using the MQTT bridge we've set up.

Remote Sensor Reading

Publisher Node (remote_sensor.py):

```python
import rospy
from std_msgs.msg import Float64
import paho.mqtt.client as mqtt


def on_connect(client, userdata, flags, rc):
    print("Connected with result code "+str(rc))
```

```python
    client.subscribe("ros_iot_topic")

def on_message(client, userdata, msg):
    print(msg.payload)

def sensor_publish():
    rospy.init_node('remote_sensor', anonymous=True)
    pub = rospy.Publisher('/remote/sensor/data', Float64, queue_size=10)
    rate = rospy.Rate(1) # 1 Hz

    client = mqtt.Client()
    client.on_connect = on_connect
    client.connect("robomq.ros.rosbridge.io", 1883, 60)

    while not rospy.is_shutdown():
        data = random.uniform(-10, 10) # simulate sensor data
        pub.publish(data)
        client.publish("ros_iot_topic", str(data))
        rate.sleep()

if __name__ == '__main__':
    try:
        sensor_publish()
    except rospy.ROSInterruptException:
        pass
```

Remote Actuator Control

Subscriber Node (remote_actuator.py):

```python
import rospy
from std_msgs.msg import Float64
import paho.mqtt.client as mqtt
```

```python
def on_connect(client, userdata, flags, rc):
    print("Connected with result code "+str(rc))
    client.subscribe("/remote/sensor/data")


def on_message(client, userdata, msg):
    data = float(msg.payload)
    if data > 0:
        # control actuator based on sensor data
        pass


def actuator_subscribe():
    rospy.init_node('remote_actuator', anonymous=True)

    client = mqtt.Client()
    client.on_connect = on_connect
    client.connect("robomq.ros.rosbridge.io", 1883, 60)

    while not rospy.is_shutdown():
        client.loop()


if __name__ == '__main__':
    try:
        actuator_subscribe()
    except rospy.ROSInterruptException:
        pass
```

Chapter 22: ROS2 Migration and Features

Introduction to ROS2

ROS2 is the next generation robot operating system that builds upon the success of ROS. It introduces several improvements and new features while maintaining backward compatibility with ROS1 where possible.

Differences between ROS and ROS2

Node Management

In ROS, nodes are managed by roscore. In ROS2, there's no centralized node manager. Instead, nodes can launch themselves or use tools like ros2 run.

Communication Protocols

ROS uses TCP/IP for communication while ROS2 uses a publish/subscribe paradigm with DDS (Data Distribution Service) as the underlying middleware.

Topics vs. Services/Action Clients

In ROS2, topics are similar to ROS but services and action clients have been merged into one interface called **Services**. The distinction between ROS services and action servers has been removed in ROS2.

Writing ROS2 Nodes in Python

Here's a simple example of a ROS2 node in Python that publishes messages:

```python
import rclpy
from rclpy.node import Node
from std_msgs.msg import String


class MinimalPublisher(Node):
    def __init__(self):
```

```python
        super().__init__('minimal_publisher')
        self.publisher_ = self.create_publisher(String, 'topic', 10)
        timer_period = 0.5
        self.timer = self.create_timer(timer_period, self.timer_callback)

    def timer_callback(self):
        msg = String()
        msg.data = "Hello World: %s" % self.get_clock().now()
        self.publisher_.publish(msg)

def main(args=None):
    rclpy.init(args=args)
    minimal_publisher = MinimalPublisher()
    rclpy.spin(minimal_publisher)
    minimal_publisher.destroy_node()
    rclpy.shutdown()

if __name__ == '__main__':
    main()
```

Migrating Python-based ROS Projects to ROS2

To migrate a ROS1 project, follow these steps:

1. **Install ROS2**: Ensure you have installed ROS2 and sourced the setup file.

2. **Update Dependencies**:

    – Change your catkin_make command to colcon build.

    – Update your dependencies using ament_index.yml instead of package.xml.

3. **Rewrite ROS Nodes**:

    – Rewrite your nodes following ROS2 conventions.

- Replace ROS1 APIs with ROS2 APIs.

Here's an example of migrating a simple ROS node:

```python
// ROS1 node
#!/usr/bin/env python
import rospy
from std_msgs.msg import String


def callback(data):
    rospy.loginfo("I heard %s", data.data)


def listener():
    rospy.init_node('listener', anonymous=True)
    rospy.Subscriber("chatter", String, callback)


if __name__ == '__main__':
    listener()
```

Migrated ROS2 node:

```python
// ROS2 node
#!/usr/bin/env python
import rclpy
from rclpy.node import Node
from std_msgs.msg import String


class Listener(Node):
    def __init__(self):
        super().__init__('listener')
        self.subscriber_ = self.create_subscription(String, 'chatter', self.callback, 10)

    def callback(self, msg: String):
```

```python
        self.get_logger().info('I heard %s', msg.data)


def main(args=None):
    rclpy.init(args=args)
    listener = Listener()
    rclpy.spin(listener)
    listener.destroy_node()
    rclpy.shutdown()


if __name__ == '__main__':
    main()
```

Practical Examples of Using Python in ROS2

Service Clients

Here's an example of a ROS2 service client in Python:

```python
import rclpy
from rclpy.node import Node
from shape_msgs.msg import Shape
from geometry_msgs.msg import Point
from shapes_srv.srv import AddShapes


class ServiceClient(Node):
    def __init__(self):
        super().__init__('service_client')
        self.client = self.create_client(AddShapes, 'add_shapes')

    def send_request(self):
        req = Shape()
        req.type = Shape.CIRCLE
        req.points.append(Point(x=1.0))
```

```python
        req.color.r = 0.5

        future = self.client.call_async(req)
        rclpy.spin_until_future_complete(self, future)

        if future.result() is not None:
            response = future.result()
            self.get_logger().info('Response: %s', str(response))

def main(args=None):
    rclpy.init(args=args)
    service_client = ServiceClient()
    service_client.send_request()
    rclpy.shutdown()

if __name__ == '__main__':
    main()
```

Chapter 23: Deployment and Optimization

In this chapter, we will explore how to deploy Python-based ROS (Robot Operating System) applications on robots, optimize performance for Python nodes, and discuss best practices for deploying ROS systems in production environments.

Deploying Python-based ROS Applications on Robots

Before deploying your application, ensure that the robot hardware platform you're targeting supports ROS. Here are simple steps using catkin workspace as an example:

1. **Create a catkin workspace**: If you haven't already, create a ROS workspace and navigate to it:

    ```
    mkdir -p ~/ros_catkin_ws/src
    cd ~/ros_catkin_ws/
    ```

2. **Copy your Python package**: Assume you have created a Python-based ROS package named my_package using the ROS package generator (catkin_create_pkg). Copy this package to the src folder:

    ```
    cp -r ~/path/to/my_package/src
    ```

3. **Build and source your workspace**:

    ```
    catkin_make
    source devel/setup.bash
    ```

4. **Deploy on the robot**: You can now deploy your application on the robot by copying the entire ROS workspace to the target machine:

    ```
    scp -r ~/ros_catkin_ws/ user@robot_ip:~/
    ```

5. **Run your node**: Finally, navigate to the workspace and source it before running your Python node:

```
cd ~/ros_catkin_ws/
source devel/setup.bash
rosrun my_package my_node.py
```

Optimizing Python Nodes for Performance

Python is an interpreted language, which can impact performance. Here are some tips to optimize your ROS Python nodes:

1. **Avoid global Interrupt (CTRL+C)**: Using signal or atexit to handle shutdowns gracefully can improve performance.

   ```python
   import signal
   import atexit

   def sigint_handler(sig, frame):
       print("Received Ctrl-C!")


   signal.signal(signal.SIGINT, sigint_handler)
   ```

2. **Use efficient data structures**: ROS messages are already optimized for publishing and subscribing. Stick to standard types like std_msgs/Float64 or std_msgs/String unless you have a specific reason not to.

3. **Avoid unnecessary computations**: Reduce computation inside your callback functions as much as possible. If possible, move heavy computations to other nodes or use external libraries optimized for performance (e.g., NumPy).

Best Practices for Deploying ROS Systems in Production

When deploying ROS systems in production environments, consider these best practices:

1. **Modularize your code**: Break down complex tasks into smaller, independent modules/packages. This improves maintainability and allows for easier scaling.

2. **Version control**: Use Git or other version control systems to track changes and enable collaboration among team members.

3. **Automate deployment**: Use tools like catkin with colcon to automate the build process, and infrastructure-as-code (IaC) tools like Docker or Kubernetes for automated deployment.

4. **Use ROS 2**: ROS 2 is designed to be more robust, scalable, and secure than ROS. It supports better real-time capabilities, DDS middleware, and improves performance with large-scale systems.

5. **Monitor your system**: Implement logging and monitoring solutions (e.g., rosbag, rostopic echo, rqt_graph) to track the health of your ROS nodes and entire system.

6. **Test thoroughly**: Develop a comprehensive testing strategy that covers edge cases, failures, and recovery scenarios to ensure robustness in production environments.

Chapter 24: Advanced Robotics Applications

In this chapter, we will explore advanced robotics applications using Python and ROS (Robot Operating System). We will focus on case studies in industrial robotics, building autonomous drones, and practical examples of complex robotic systems.

Case Studies: Python in Industrial Robotics

Python's simplicity and extensive library support make it a popular choice for industrial robotics. Let's look at two concise case studies:

Example 1: Pick-and-Place with MoveIt!

MoveIt! is a ROS package that enables smooth robot motion planning and execution. We'll use Python and MoveIt! to create a pick-and-place task using a dual-arm robotic manipulator like the UR5e.

```python
import moveit_commander
import numpy as np


# Initialize MoveIt Commander
moveit_commander.roscpp_initialize([])
robot = moveit_commander.RobotCommander()
scene = moveit_commander.PlanningSceneInterface()


# Define pick-and-place locations (Cartesian coordinates)
pick_location = np.array([0.2, 0.2, 0.1])
place_location = np.array([0.4, 0.3, 0.1])


# Move robot to pick location
robot.set_pose_target(pick_location)
plan = robot.plan()
robot.go(wait=True)
```

```python
# Execute picking task here (e.g., using a gripper interface)

# Move robot to place location
robot.set_pose_target(place_location)
plan = robot.plan()
robot.go(wait=True)

# Execute placing task here (e.g., releasing the object)
```

Example 2: Quality Control Inspection with OpenCV

OpenCV is a popular computer vision library that can be used for quality control tasks in industrial robotics. Let's use Python and OpenCV to perform an object detection task on a conveyor belt.

```python
import cv2
import numpy as np

# Initialize camera and grab image
cap = cv2.VideoCapture(0)
ret, frame = cap.read()

# Convert to grayscale and apply Gaussian blur
gray = cv2.cvtColor(frame, cv2.COLOR_BGR2GRAY)
blur = cv2.GaussianBlur(gray, (5, 5), 0)

# Perform edge detection using Canny
edges = cv2.Canny(blur, 50, 150)

# Find contours and filter by area
contours, _ = cv2.findContours(edges, cv2.RETR_EXTERNAL,
cv2.CHAIN_APPROX_SIMPLE)
good_contours = [c for c in contours if cv2.contourArea(c) > 100]
```

```python
# Draw bounding boxes around detected objects
for cnt in good_contours:
    x, y, w, h = cv2.boundingRect(cnt)
    cv2.rectangle(frame, (x, y), (x + w, y + h), (0, 255, 0), 2)

# Display result
cv2.imshow('Frame', frame)
cv2.waitKey(0)
cv2.destroyAllWindows()
```

ROS is widely used in drone development due to its support for multi-vehicle coordination and sensor fusion. Let's build a simple autonomous drone using the PX4 flight stack, Gazebo simulation, and Python-based controllers.

Example 1: Offboard Control

Offboard control allows us to use a ground station computer to control a drone remotely via ROS. Here's how to create an offboard controller using the mavros package:

```python
import rospy
from geometry_msgs.msg import PoseStamped

# Initialize node and services
rospy.init_node('offboard_control')
local_pos_pub = rospy.Publisher('/mavros/setpoint_position/local', PoseStamped, queue_size=10)

# Define desired position
pose = PoseStamped()
pose.header.frame_id = 'map'
pose.pose.position.x = 5.0
```

```python
pose.pose.position.y = 5.0
pose.pose.position.z = 2.0


rate = rospy.Rate(10) # Control frequency in Hz


# Publish desired position to local position controller
while not rospy.is_shutdown():
    pose.header.stamp = rospy.Time.now()
    local_pos_pub.publish(pose)
    rate.sleep()
```

Example 2: Autonomous Navigation

To enable autonomous navigation, we'll use the navfn package for planning missions and the crazyflie_ros package for controlling a Crazyflie 2.0 micro-drone.

```python
import rospy
from navfn import NavFn


# Initialize node and services
rospy.init_node('autonomous_navigation')
nav = NavFn()


# Define waypoints
waypoints = [(0, 0), (1, 1), (-1, -1)]


# Plan mission using NavFn
mission = nav.generate(waypoints)


# Publish mission to Crazyflie controller
for wp in mission:
    # Assuming 'cf' is your Crazyflie ROS interface instance
    cf.send_waypoint(wp)
```

In this section, we'll explore two practical examples of advanced robotic systems using Python and ROS.

Example 1: Collaborative Robot (Cobot) Task Execution

Collaborative robots like the Universal Robots UR series can be programmed using ROS to perform complex tasks in cooperation with other robots or humans. Let's use Python and MoveIt! to demonstrate a simple cobot task execution scenario involving pick-and-place operations.

```python
import moveit_commander
import numpy as np


# Initialize MoveIt Commander for cobot
moveit_commander.roscpp_initialize([])
robot = moveit_commander.RobotCommander()
scene = moveit_commander.PlanningSceneInterface()


# Define pick-and-place locations (Cartesian coordinates)
pick_location = np.array([0.2, 0.2, 0.1])
place_location = np.array([0.4, 0.3, 0.1])


# Move cobot to pick location
robot.set_pose_target(pick_location)
plan = robot.plan()
robot.go(wait=True)


# Execute picking task here (e.g., using a gripper interface)


# Move cobot to place location
robot.set_pose_target(place_location)
```

```
plan = robot.plan()
robot.go(wait=True)
```

Execute placing task here (e.g., releasing the object)

Example 2: Multi-Robot Collaboration

Multi-robot systems require coordination, communication, and task allocation. Let's use ROS to demonstrate a simple multi-robot foraging task using two differential-drive robots like the TurtleBot.

```python
import rospy
from geometry_msgs.msg import Twist

# Initialize nodes for each robot
rospy.init_node('robot_1')
cmd_pub_1 = rospy.Publisher('/robot_1/cmd_vel', Twist, queue_size=10)

rospy.init_node('robot_2')
cmd_pub_2 = rospy.Publisher('/robot_2/cmd_vel', Twist, queue_size=10)

rate = rospy.Rate(10) # Control frequency in Hz

# Define foraging task function
def forage():
    twist = Twist()
    twist.linear.x = 0.15 # Set linear speed
    twist.angular.z = 0.2 # Set angular speed (random exploration)
    return twist

# Publish commands to each robot's velocity controller
while not rospy.is_shutdown():
    cmd_1 = forage()
```

```
cmd_pub_1.publish(cmd_1)

cmd_2 = forage()
cmd_pub_2.publish(cmd_2)

rate.sleep()
```

These examples demonstrate the versatility of Python and ROS in advanced robotics applications. By combining these tools with appropriate libraries, sensors, and hardware platforms, developers can create sophisticated robotic systems tailored to specific tasks and environments.

Chapter 25: Community and Resources

Exploring Python-based ROS Packages

The Robot Operating System (ROS) ecosystem is vast and continuously growing. Many packages available in ROS are implemented using Python due to its simplicity, readability, and powerful libraries. To explore these packages, you can use the rospack command-line tool or query the ROS Wiki.

Here's how to search for Python-based ROS packages:

$ rospack find --python <package_name>

For example, to find Python packages related to sensors:

$ rospack find --python sensor*

You can also explore packages on the ROS Wiki by navigating to the Packages page and filtering by language using the sidebar menu.

Contributing to Open-Source ROS Projects

Contributing to open-source projects is a great way to learn, improve your skills, and give back to the community. Many ROS packages are open-source and welcome contributions. Here's how you can get started:

1. **Fork** the desired package repository on GitHub.
2. **Clone** your fork locally: git clone https://github.com/your_username/package_name.git
3. **Create a new branch** for your feature or fix: git checkout -b new-feature
4. **Make changes**, following the project's coding style and commit conventions.
5. **Commit** your changes with meaningful messages.
6. **Push** your branch to your fork on GitHub.
7. Submit a **pull request (PR)** from your fork's branch to the original repository.

Before contributing, make sure you have read and understood the project's README file and contribution guidelines.

Here's an example of improving the documentation for a ROS package:

```
$ cd catkin_ws/src/package_name
$ touch README.md  # Create a new markdown file for README
$ git add README.md  # Stage the new file for commit
$ git commit -m "Update README with more information"  # Commit with a meaningful message
$ git push origin your-branch-name  # Push changes to your fork's branch
```

The ROS community maintains several resources that can help you learn, troubleshoot, and stay updated. Here are some essential ones:

1. **ROS Wiki**: The official ROS Wiki is the primary source of information about ROS, including tutorials, packages, and documentation.

2. **Stack Overflow**: Many ROS-related questions are answered on Stack Overflow with the ROS tag: https://stackoverflow.com/questions/tagged/ros

3. **ROS Answers**: This platform is dedicated to answering ROS-specific questions: http://answers.ros.org/

4. **GitHub**: Many ROS packages are hosted on GitHub, and their issue trackers can provide insights into usage and development.

By staying engaged with the community and regularly checking these resources, you'll be well-informed about the latest developments in ROS and Python for robotics.